THE FORMATION
OF KAZAKH
IDENTITY

The Former Soviet South project is sponsored by:

- A. Meredith Jones & Co. Ltd
- B.A.T Industries plc
- The British Petroleum Company plc
- ENI S.p.A.
- John Laing International Limited
- Statoil

Series editor: Edmund Herzig

The Royal Institute of International Affairs is an independent body which promotes the rigorous study of international questions and does not express opinions of its own. The opinions expressed in this publication are the responsibility of the author.

FORMER SOVIET SOUTH PROJECT

THE FORMATION OF KAZAKH IDENTITY

From Tribe to Nation-State

Shirin Akiner

THE ROYAL INSTITUTE OF
INTERNATIONAL AFFAIRS
Russian and CIS Programme

© Royal Institute of International Affairs, 1995

Published in Great Britain in 1995 by the Royal Institute of International Affairs,
Chatham House, 10 St James's Square, London SW1Y 4LE
(Charity Registration No. 208 223)

Distributed worldwide by The Brookings Institution, 1775 Massachusetts Avenue, NW,
Washington, DC 20036-2188, USA.

All rights reserved. No part of this publication may be reproduced, stored in a retrieval system, or transmitted by any other means without the prior written permission of the copyright holder. Please direct all inquiries to the publishers.

ISBN 1 899658 03 3

Printed and bound in Great Britain by the Chameleon Press Ltd
Cover design by Youngs Design in Production

CONTENTS

About the author vii
Summary viii

1 Introduction 1
2 Background 5
3 History 8
4 Sovietization 34
5 Rediscovery and redefinition: towards a new national identity 51
6 Independent Kazakhstan 60
7 Conclusion 80

Further reading 83

ABOUT THE AUTHOR

Dr Shirin Akiner is Director of the Central Asia Research Forum at the School of Oriental and African Studies, University of London. She convenes and teaches courses relating to Central Asia at undergraduate and postgraduate level. She has long first-hand experience of the region and speaks several of the indigenous languages. She has directed five British government-funded training projects with Kazakhstan and Uzbekistan, and acted as consultant for several award-winning radio and television documentaries. Her publications include: *Islamic Peoples of the Soviet Union*, Kegan Paul International, 1983, revised 1987; *Mongolia Today* (ed.), KPI, 1990; *Cultural Tradition and Change in Central Asia* (ed.), KPI, 1991; *Central Asia: New Arc of Conflict?* Royal United Services Institute for Defence Studies, 1993; *Political and Economic Trends in Central Asia* (ed.), British Academic Press, 1994; *Resistance and Reform in Tibet* (ed. with R. Barnett), Indiana University Press, 1994. Dr Akiner is the editor of the monthly news bulletin *Central Asia Newsfile* and *Labyrinth: the Central Asia Quarterly,* both published by the Central Asia Research Forum.

SUMMARY

Kazakh society has undergone two major transformations in the past century and a half: first, incorporation into the Russian empire and exposure to European culture under Tsarist rule, then the ruthless and massive social, economic and cultural restructuring under Soviet power. Both of these have fundamentally altered notions of personal and collective identity. Today, as an independent nation, the Kazakhs are embarking on the difficult process of reinterpreting a history and a culture that are fraught with fracture and ambiguity, and developing an identity appropriate to capitalism and the twenty-first century. This process is not taking place in a vacuum, but as a concomitant of profound social and economic change.

The situation is further complicated by the fact that the Kazakhs, as the titular people of Kazakhstan, have suddenly and unexpectedly acquired a degree of control over, and responsibility for, a large number of non-Kazakh minorities. The radically multi-ethnic nature of Kazakhstan is one of the most important factors contributing to the moulding of a post-Soviet Kazakh identity. Arguably, the most crucial issue on the political agenda of Kazakhstan today is to what extent and in what form a specifically Kazakh national identity will be able to coexist with an overarching multi-ethnic Kazakhstani identity.

This study examines in detail the historical factors that have contributed to the formation of Kazakh identity, and shows how they inform the current debate on 'Kazakh-ness' and how this in turn will impact on the future of Kazakhstan.

1 INTRODUCTION

Kazakhstan, the second largest state in the CIS, and one of those most liberally endowed with natural resources, was initially regarded as the most stable. In this nation of minorities, no single one of which had an overall majority, it seemed, at first, as though a truly multi-ethnic state was being created, one in which all the different groups had an equal stake, based on equal opportunities and equal rights. This outlook was encapsulated in the term 'Kazakhstani', which encompassed all the citizens of the new state, with no ethnic bias. It soon became clear, however, that political independence had given new emphasis to the question of Kazakh identity: what was its history, what were its defining features, what should be its role in contemporary society? Arguably, the most crucial issues on the political agenda of Kazakhstan today are precisely these: to what extent, and in what form, a specifically Kazakh national identity will be able to coexist with an overarching multi-ethnic, multicultural Kazakhstani identity. It is possible that a solution will be found that accommodates the aspirations of the titular Kazakh group as well as those of other minorities: in this case, it is likely that Kazakhstan will be able to realize its undeniable social and economic potential; if not, then instability, strife and territorial fragmentation are almost inevitable.

Neither the (Kazakh) nation-building nor (Kazakhstani) state-building projects are as yet far enough advanced for the probable course of events to be predicted with any degree of certainty. What is possible, however, is to identify the factors that have contributed to the formation of modern Kazakh self-perceptions. These have an extraordinarily complex background: some are the product of the Soviet experience, some have their origins in a distant past. The situation is further complicated by the fact that Kazakh society has undergone two major transformations over the past century and a half: first, under the Tsarist regime, the Europeanization/Russification of a large proportion of the Kazakh aristocracy, as well as far-reaching administrative and economic changes; and secondly, under the Soviet regime, the total destruction of the nomadic way of life and the coopting of the intellectual political elites into the new system. Today, the Kazakhs are confronted not only with a multitude of practical problems that are directly connected with the sudden and unexpected acquisition of independence, but also with the need to knit together the disparate, fractured parts of their history.

The rupture between modern and pre-modern Kazakh history was so profound that to most non-Kazakhs the links between the two often seem tenuous to the point of insignificance. To Kazakhs, however, re-establishing a sense of continuity, in their own eyes as well as in the way in which they are perceived by others, is a matter of vital importance. Without this, they would be rootless, nothing other than the products of Soviet social and cultural engineering; by extension, they would have no historical legitimacy and thus no legitimate territorial or national claims. Far from being a romantic fantasy, their current preoccupation with the whole sweep of Kazakh history, projected back over some 2,000 years, is therefore of very real political relevance, relating to immediate concerns regarding national and territorial survival. This in large measure explains the urgency, obsessive passion, and occasional disregard of the sensitivities of other ethnic groups that not infrequently characterize the behaviour of the more radical sections of contemporary Kazakh society. Yet the reconstruction of the national myth is in itself a matter of dispute: different factions give prominence to different events and different tendencies. Thus, there is no consensus as to what constitute the defining features of the national identity.

Perceptions of identity are shaped primarily by a desire to demarcate boundaries between 'us/me' and 'them/others'. They operate on many different planes, from the domestic to the global, from the ephemeral (e.g. membership of a club) to the seemingly eternal (e.g. adherence to a religious faith); also on a scale that ranges from that of an individual to that of a community of any size that the imagination can encompass. Some identities are inherited, some chosen for strategic advantage, some imposed by majorities on minorities. Each unit, whether it be a single person, a group, or a conglomeration of entities, is capable of concurrently maintaining an array of different, at times even apparently mutually incompatible identities, whose hierarchical ranking and active potency are determined by the parameters of a given situation.

Questions relating to concepts of identity have long been the subject of academic as well as popular interest. Over the past couple of decades, however, it is identity as expressed through ethnicity and nationalism that has attracted an unprecedented level of attention. These two aspects are closely linked and at times overlap. Usage and terminological definition vary from one writer to another, depending on their points of reference. In very broad outline, the former term is generally taken to refer to a cultural category (although 'ethnic group' is commonly used as a euphemism for minorities of a different 'racial' background), while the latter, to use Ernest Gellner's thesis, 'is primarily a political principle, which holds that the political and the national unit should be congruent'. The precise definitions of these terms may differ, but the one point that is clear is that they both refer to a sense of collective identity, based on various norms of cultural/social/physical differentiation, which in turn represent perceived criteria for inclusion and exclusion from a given group. This does not necessarily have to result in conflict: in many societies there has been, and still continues to be, a recognition of group differences within a mutually acceptable framework of peaceful political coexistence. However, there is always the possibility that perceived differences may be mobilized in such a way as to cause strife.

This has, indeed, become an all-too-familiar pattern in recent years. Most of the armed conflicts in the post-Second World War era have been rooted in a heightened projection of ethnic and/or national issues. One of the chief reasons for this is that in the states that were born out of the dissolution of colonial empires – first those of the west European countries, then the Communist bloc – ethnic and national identity have been used as building bricks in the process of establishing political cohesion. Great emphasis has been placed on such 'consolidating' features as a shared history, shared language and shared culture. Since 'shared' in such cases almost always refers to the attributes of the majority (or the largest and most powerful minority), it has inevitably created resentment and insecurity among the excluded, marginalized sectors of the population. In some cases this has resulted in constant, but low-level, terrorist activity; in others it has exploded into open warfare. More often than not, neighbouring states are sucked into such conflicts, either as the involuntary recipients of floods of refugees, or, if there are cross-border ethnic links, as active participants.

Will Kazakhstan contribute to regional tensions by fostering ethnic confrontation, or will it succeed in developing a model of ethnic harmony? The answer to this question must in large measure depend on the form in which the Kazakhs, the titular and dominant people of the republic, assert their national identity.

This study of the formation of Kazakh national identity (which is restricted to the Kazakhs of Kazakhstan) takes the form of a historical narrative. This may seem an unnecessarily circuitous way of approaching a contemporary topic. However, there are a number of reasons why, in this case, it is justified. First, as indicated above, many of the political as well as cultural debates are rooted in arguments that relate to the past – at times, indeed, an almost mythical past; thus, for example, the question as to whether, in the 1995 Constitution, Kazakhstan should be referred to as 'the ancient Kazakh land' or 'the primordial Kazakh land' was based on an interpretation of prehistoric material. Secondly, Kazakh history has been subjected to so many revisions that it is not possible to single out any one source as a comprehensive, reasonably objective guide; yet without an established frame of reference it is almost impossible to evaluate key processes such as, for example, the possibility (or otherwise) of a revival of Horde rivalry, or the oscillation between alienation and rapprochement that marks the relationship with Russia. Thirdly, there is the vexed question of the nomad legacy: sedentary, literate communities can locate their history in datable charters, registers, buildings, and works of art and craft. Nomads have none of this; their history is recorded, precariously, in oral traditions and the accounts of 'outsiders'. Yet this lack of visibility does not mean that the nomad past can be ignored: on the contrary, it is essential that it be taken into account in any attempt to understand modern Kazakh identity, since it continues to exert a strong symbolic influence, informing present perceptions of self-definition. Finally, the process of creating a post-Soviet Kazakh national identity is still at a very early stage: neither the historical approach nor any other form of analysis can yet provide clear answers as to where it is leading. However, the historical narrative can help to illuminate some of the underlying factors and thereby to give a deeper understanding of current trends in the process.

2 BACKGROUND

The area which traditionally constituted 'Kazakh lands', over which the Kazakhs pursued their seasonal cycle of migration, was somewhat larger than that encompassed by present-day Kazakhstan. At its largest extent, it stretched from the lower reaches of the Volga river and the Caspian Sea in the west to the Tarim and Ili rivers in the east, from the lower margin of Siberia in the north to the Syr Darya and Chu rivers in the south (see map overleaf). It is a region that presents few obstacles to human movement other than sheer size (it covers approximately 3 million square kilometres) and, in parts, a shortage of water and sparse vegetation. For centuries, the boundaries were fluid, imposed not by natural constraints, but by the might and rapacity of rival nomad neighbours. From the eighteenth century onwards, however, the Russian and Chinese empires steadily extended their respective frontiers into the Central Asian interior, gradually hemming in the Kazakhs and other nomadic peoples, setting fixed limits to their territory and curbing their mobility.

The environment dictated the tenor of nomad life, as well as the contours of the tribal 'horde' territories. Even today, after sedentarization and over sixty years of intensive modernization, the environment still plays a decisive role in the life of the modern Kazakh state: the distances remain a challenge to be overcome; the mineral wealth a promise to be realized; the scale and beauty of the landscape a backdrop to everyday life; the ecology a cause for concern. Above all, the land itself is seen as part of the national identity, the link between past and present.

The physical relief of the region falls into four zones.[1] In the north, down to the level of Turgai and Semipalatinsk, there is a belt of steppe, a continuation of the Western Siberian plain. The winters here are long, lasting five to six months, and cold, with the temperatures dropping as low as –45°C. Summer lasts less than three months. There are hundreds of lakes in this region, and several rivers, the largest being the Irtysh, Ishim and Tobol, which flow northwards, and the Ural, which flows southward to empty into the Caspian Sea.

---

1 The best description in English of the physical geography of the region is given by S.P. Suslov, *Physical Geography of Asiatic Russia*, transl. N.D. Gershevsky (San Francisco, Freeman and Co., 1961).

Approximate Territorial Limits of Kazakh Hordes c. 1750

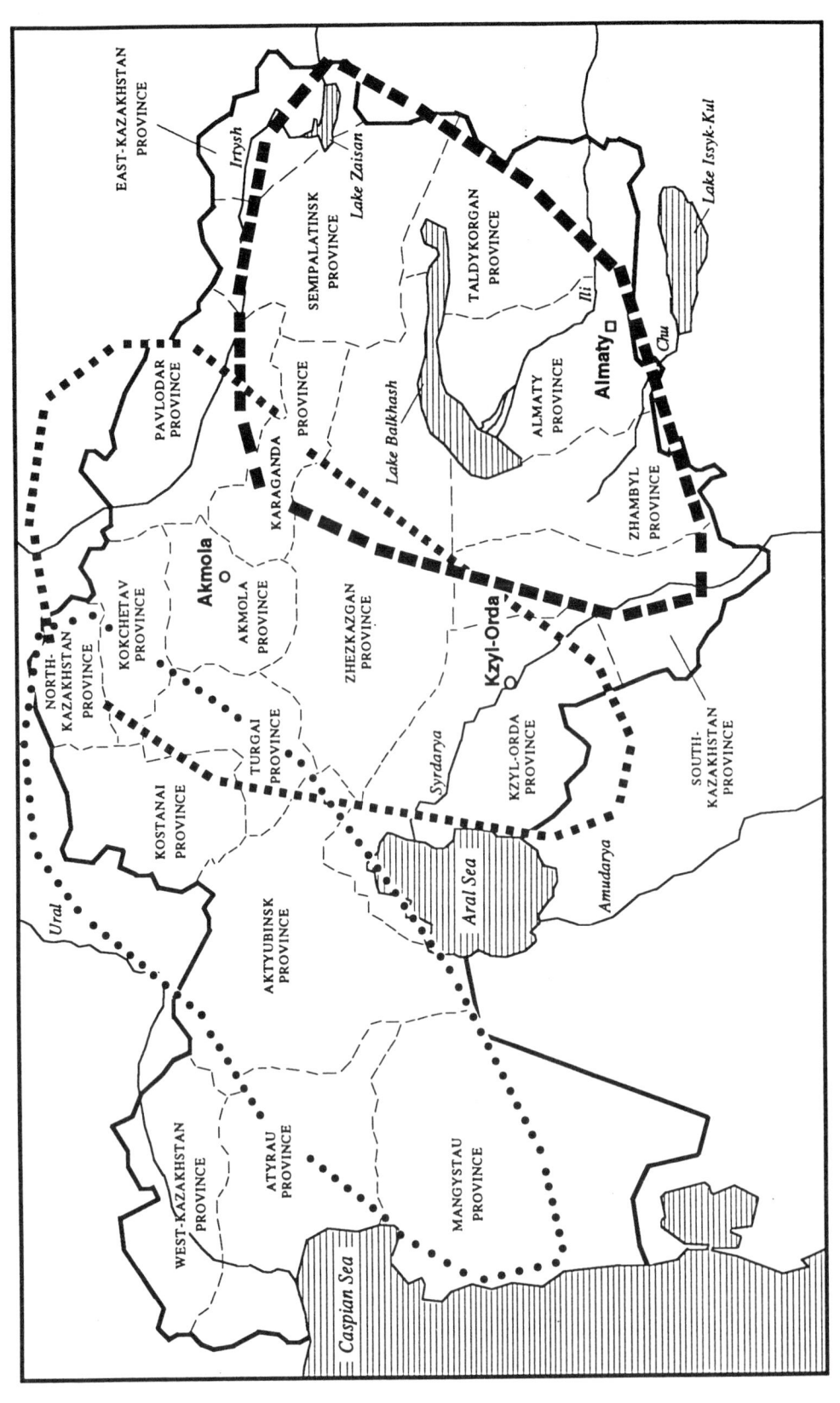

Key to map:
- ▬ ▬ ▬ - Big Horde
- ▬ ▬ ▬ - Middle Horde
- ••••••• - Little Horde

The central zone is occupied by a broad band of semi-desert, stretching from the river Emba to Lake Zaisan. The land slopes steeply down from the uplands of the east and centre to the Caspian Sea depression, much of which lies well below sea level, in the west. The rolling hills and plateaux that lie between the Ulu-Tau and the Altai mountains are known as the 'Kazakh Folded Country'. Here there are major deposits of coal (particularly in the Karaganda region) and metallic ores. Further to the west, there are vast deposits of hydrocarbons. The semi-desert has plentiful but inconstant sources of water. There are numerous lakes (some freshwater, some salt), but many dry up in the summer. Several of the smaller, shallower rivers also flow only in the spring. The annual as well as the daily variation of temperature in this central region is very considerable and precipitation is low. Throughout the year the region is scoured by strong winds. In winter, blizzards are not uncommon, but the snow cover is usually swept away very rapidly, allowing animals pastured in the open to continue foraging. The weather conditions that the nomads dreaded the most were a thaw followed by a sudden freeze, known as *zhut*. This causes a hard, clear layer of ice to form through which the animals can see, but not reach, their feed. Often, a very large area will be affected by zhut. Even today, with modern equipment at hand, it can cause devastation. In the past, it meant the inevitable death of tens, even hundreds, of thousands of head of livestock. Not surprisingly, the years of the great zhut are etched in the folk memory – historic landmarks which act as points of reference for lesser events.

To the south, between the Caspian Sea and Lake Balkhash, lies the desert zone. The climate is very dry and there is a serious water deficit. Precipitation measures 100 millimetres or less per annum; water losses through evaporation are very high. The five summer months are cloudless, with a midday maximum temperature that can rise as high as 45°C. The littoral belt of the Caspian Sea, however, has a milder climate. The river valleys, too, have their own microclimates and in summer are distinctly cooler than the open desert. The region is subject to intense seismic activity, especially in the southwest, where an average of 1,000 earthquakes are registered each year.

Finally, in the south and southeast, there is the mountain zone, formed by the Altai and Tien Shan ranges. In places, these rise to peaks of 2,500 metres and above. The lower slopes are covered with deciduous woods; in the south, there are extensive walnut groves, also wild almonds, vines and many different types of apple (which, in the twentieth century, gave rise to the understandable but erroneous etymology of 'Alma-Ata' as the 'Father of Apples'). Higher up, these give way to coniferous forests. Above the tree line there are subalpine and alpine meadows, which provide superb pasturage in the summer months.

3 HISTORY

Origins

The origins of the Kazakhs are unclear. Physically, they are classified as South Siberian Mongoloid, but the Kazakh language belongs to the central Turkic family. The vocabulary contains a significant proportion of early loans from Arabic, Persian and Mongol, and a more recent stratum of Russian loans. Dialectal divergences are relatively few in number and slight.

What is difficult to establish is the historical sequence of events that led to the ethnogenesis of this group. Folk tradition traces the origins of the Kazakhs back to a single legendary progenitor named Alash(a)-khan. Modern historians reject that explanation, but there is no unanimity of opinion as to whether the Kazakhs of today are predominantly the descendants of incomers, possibly of the fifteenth century or later, or whether they are representatives of an ethnic continuum that has been present in the region for several millennia. The desire to establish roots, to construct a national narrative that firmly links the modern Kazakhs to the territory of Kazakhstan, has made even the study of prehistory a highly political issue. The absence of Kazakh written records means that, until the nineteenth century, the chief sources of information were the treaties, chronicles, travellers' accounts and other such documents compiled by their sedentary neighbours. These are of great importance for the study of Kazakh history, but there is inevitably the danger that they may contain inaccurate information, the result of misunderstandings, lack of first-hand knowledge or deliberately hostile propaganda. Moreover, especially for the earliest period, the material is so fragmentary that its interpretation is usually highly speculative. Given that there is so little concrete, verifiable information, theories concerning the origins of the Kazakhs tend to be rooted at least as much in political concerns as in objective historical research.

Earliest inhabitants: Sakas to Turks

Archaeologists have identified the remains of some 200 neolithic settlements, distributed all over the territory of present-day Kazakhstan. By the middle of the second millennium BC the working of metallic ores was well developed, and technically accomplished copper and bronze artefacts were being produced. The inhabitants of the region at this period seem to have been sedentary agriculturists and livestock-breeders. In the first millennium BC nomadic tribes made their appearance. The best documented of these are the Sakas, a tribal confederation that dominated southern Kazakhstan from around the seventh to the fourth centuries BC.[2] In the third century BC new groups of nomadic pastoralists moved into the region, merging with the Sakas and, it would seem, adopting much of their culture. The three tribes that are of most significance for later Kazakh history are the Usuns, Kangyu and Alans; some Kazakh historians believe that they are direct forebears of the present Kazakh people.[3] The Usuns (or possibly the Sakas) were highly skilled craftsmen, as is evidenced by the large number of tools, utensils, weapons and ornaments that have survived from this period.

Some Soviet scholars (and not only Kazakhs) contended that there was a Turkic-speaking presence in Central Asia before the end of the first millennium BC. Most Western Turkologists, however, date the first appearance of a Turkic people in this region to the sixth century AD, when the tribal confederation known as the Turkic Kaghanate (or alternatively, the Gök Türk empire) was established in the territory of southern Kazakhstan, Transoxiana and the Altai mountains.

Mongols

In the early thirteenth century Genghiz Khan and his Mongol hordes swept into Central Asia, capturing the oasis cities of Transoxiana, among them Otrar and Taraz in the territory of present-day southern Kazakhstan. The Mongols then proceeded to fan out to the north, south and west, conquering large swathes of Europe, Transcaucasia and the Middle East. Genghiz Khan divided this huge empire between his sons. The lands to the west, which included the Aral Sea, central Russia and Siberia, formed the *Ulus* ('appanage') of Dzhuchi, his eldest son. In the first half of the fourteenth century this state, which came to be known as the 'Golden Horde', began to disintegrate into semi-autonomous sub-groupings. A similar process of disintegration took place in the Ulus of Chagatai, Genghiz Khan's second son, which occupied the territory to the east of the Golden Horde, including Transoxiana and the Tien Shan mountains as far south as Kashgar. Towards the end of the fourteenth century an independent khanate, known

---

2   *The Cambridge History of Early Inner Asia* (Cambridge, CUP, 1990) provides an authoritative introduction to the study of this period; M. Auezov *et al.* (eds), *Istoriya Kazakhskoy SSR* (*Qazaq SSR Tarikhy*), I (Alma-Ata, AN KazSSR, 1957) (hereafter *Istoriya*, I), pp. 9–52, treats the Kazakh region in more detail and is also of historiographic interest for the Soviet gloss.
3   *Istoriya*, I, p. 41.

as Mogolistan, was formed, encompassing the region that today forms part of southeastern Kazakhstan, Kyrgyzstan and northwestern Xinjiang; in the west, in Transoxiana, Tamerlane established an empire that briefly covered not only the lands of the Ulus of Chagatai, but also much of the territory of the Golden Horde, and large areas of northern India, Afghanistan, Iran and Asia Minor. In the middle of the fifteenth century, several tribal groupings in northern Mogolistan and in the vicinity of Lake Balkhash began to coalesce, eventually forming the core of what came to be known as the Kazakh Khanate. Gradually, as the Uzbek Khanate moved southwards, into the settled areas of Timurid Transoxiana, the Kazakh Khanate extended its power westwards, into the steppe regions that had formerly been held by the Uzbeks. By the early sixteenth century, the Kazakh Khanate had succeeded in gaining control of most of the territory that had formerly belonged to the White Horde, as well as the northern possessions of the Ulus of Chagatai. It has been estimated that by this time the Kazakhs numbered around one million.

During the second half of the sixteenth century the Kazakhs succeeded in wresting control of the oases and rich pastures of the Syr Darya from the Uzbeks, gaining possession of such cities as Sygnak, Otrar, Sairam, Turkestan (known as Yassy in the fourteenth to sixteenth centuries) and Tashkent. Strategically and economically these conquests were very important. They gave access to winter grazing grounds that were abundantly endowed with grasslands and thickets of reeds; they ensured control of the highly profitable trade of the cities, which provided tax revenues, a steady supply of commodities and manufactured goods, and grain from the cultivated lands of the sedentary population; not least, they provided bases that could be defended against attack, as well as serving as a springboard for further incursions into the settled areas of Turkestan. Competition amongst the Kazakh sultans for possession of these prizes was fierce; and it is conceivable that such clashes fostered the division into three separate hordes, which took place at about this time.[4]

The territorial conquests of the late sixteenth century also enhanced the influence of Islam in the nascent Kazakh state. The Kazakh khans recognized the need to secure the support of the *ulama* (senior Muslim clergy) in the cities of the south, with their long, deeply-entrenched tradition of Muslim civilization. They therefore made generous grants of *vaqf* (charitable endowments) to religious institutions. Increasingly, the sons of nobles were sent to the *madrassa* (Muslim colleges) of Transoxiana to further their education. The capture in 1598 of Turkestan, with its great Timurid mausoleum over the grave of the twelfth-century mystic, Ahmad Yasavi, made the Kazakhs guardians of one of the holiest places of pilgrimage in all Central Asia. Many Kazakh khans were later buried here, emphasizing the bond between Islam and the Kazakh rulers.

4 K. A. Pishchulina, 'Prisyrdar'inskiye goroda ... v XV-XVII vekakh', in B. Suleimenov *et al.* (eds), *Kazakhstan v XV-XVIII vekakh* (Alma-Ata, Nauka, 1969), p. 49.

On a less exalted level, itinerant preachers from the south, among them dervish masters nominally linked to Sufi orders, travelled among the Kazakh nomads, spreading the teachings of Islam, performing the necessary rituals and collecting *zakat* (religious tax). Such contacts maintained a nominal familiarity with Islamic precepts and fostered a sense of identification with the larger Muslim community, but did little to undermine the continuing practice of thinly veiled pre-Islamic customs. It was not until the nineteenth century, after annexation by Russia, that attempts were made to introduce a more rigorously orthodox approach to Islam.

Use of the term 'Kazakh'

The bulk of the population in the successor states to the Ulus of Dzhuchi and the Ulus of Chagatai consisted of Turkic, Turkicized Mongol, and possibly also pre-Mongol tribes. The constant movements of populations, resulting in the incessant merging and splintering of tribal groupings, meant that there was no clear-cut ethnic/racial division between any of these formations. In the fifteenth century, designations such as 'Uzbek' and 'Kazakh' were used very loosely, often overlapping in terms of reference. It was not until the sixteenth century that they began to assume a sharper definition.[5]

The etymology of the word 'Kazakh' remains an enigma. The folk derivation *kaz* (goose), *ak* (white), links it to the legend of a white goose (an ancient totemic symbol). Historians and philologists have not as yet succeeded in finding a more convincing explanation, though many theories have been advanced.[6] The term 'Kazakh' and similar, possibly related forms, are also found in the Caucasus and Volga-Don region from the thirteenth century onwards, but Kazakh historians firmly reject any etymological link, let alone the suggestion of a physical alliance, with the Cossacks. The matter is further confused by the fact that in Russian sources of the late sixteenth century the expression *Kazatskaya Orda* (Kazakh Horde) is used. Later, it is replaced by the terms *Kirgiz*, *Kirgiz-Kaisak*, or *Kaisak*. It is not known why this shift occurred. In the Kazakh language, however, the term *Qazaq* was used. It was not until the Soviet period that this was finally adopted as the official designation for the Kazakh people.

Finally, there is the term *Alash*. In folk tradition the personal name of the legendary founding father of the Kazakhs, Alash, has from time to time been used (sometimes in the form 'Children of Alash') as a synonym for the people as a whole.[7] In the twentieth

---

5 *Istoriya*, I, p. 142.
6 M. Tynyshpayev, *Materialy k istorii Kirgiz-Kazakskogo naroda* (Tashkent, Kirgosizdat, 1925, facsimile reproduction Alma-Ata, NB-press, 1990), pp. 31–41; *Istoriya*, I, pp. 143–4.
7 A. Atabek, *Alash i Kazakhskaya Natsiya* (Moscow, Khak, 1991), pp. 5–8; Shakarim Kudaiberdy-uly, *Rodoslovnaya Tyurkov, Kirgizov, Kazakhov i Khanskikh dinastii* (first printed Orenburg, Karimov, Khusainov and Co., 1911, reprinted in Russian translation, Alma-Ata, Dastan, 1990), p. 46.

century the term has been appropriated by Kazakh nationalists, usually those with a pan-Turkic bias, notably the Alash Orda movement and Alash party that were active on the eve of the Bolshevik revolution, and the Alash opposition group of the 1990s.

Nomadism

For over two millennia, from prehistoric times up to the twentieth century, or more precisely, up to the collectivization campaign of the Soviet period, the inhabitants of the 'Kazakh lands' followed a nomadic way of life. Although nomadism is now no longer a living tradition, it remains a fundamental element of the national self-image. The physical and mental qualities it fostered, the arts and the rituals that were connected with it, are today regarded with the same awe and veneration that is reserved, in sedentary societies, for material relics. The nomad way of life required a total dedication of time and energy and created an intimate bond between the nomad and the natural world.

Annual cycle

Animal husbandry was the chief occupation. It dictated the organizational framework of society and, in a very real sense, was the substance of nomad culture. Cattle, goats and camels were raised, but sheep and horses were the mainstay of the economy. Highly prized, these animals had complementary uses as well as a complementary symbolism. The sheep, regarded as a metaphor for the material world, provided all the basic necessities of nomad life. The strong, coarse wool could be treated in two ways: spun into yarn or felted. The yarn was used for making tent bands, thongs, bags and other such items, as well as for knitting. Felt, on the other hand, was the primary building and furnishing fabric of the circular 'beehive' *yurt* (tent). During the summer months the sheep were milked, either to satisfy immediate needs or to make cheese that would last through the winter. When the animal was finally slaughtered every morsel of flesh, gristle and other soft tissue was consumed; whatever remained was recycled for some other useful purpose. The horse was also a source of milk and meat, but its main function was as a means of transport. This mundane description, however, does not begin to do justice to the esteem in which horses in general and individual horses in particular were held. Children learned to ride before they could walk and most of the nomads' lives were spent in the saddle. Horsepower and manpower melded to give the nomads 'wings', an almost mystical bonding, celebrated in countless folk epics, proverbs and metaphors, that gave them the freedom of the inner Eurasian vastness.

The animals were pastured in the open all the year round. This required regular movement, season by season. There were four periods of transhumance. The first took place in early spring, as the snows began to melt. It lasted till April or May when a halt was made to allow for lambing, shearing and castration. The next move was to the rich summer pastures in the northern steppes, the high mountains or the river valleys. The autumn migration was completed by about October; mating, a second shearing, felt-making and other such tasks were performed at this time. The last migration, back to the more sheltered, milder winter pastures, was undertaken in late autumn. The nomads followed set routes, each group having its own hereditary grazing grounds. However, the area was so vast that there was plenty of room for manoeuvre: on each migration the precise route and the precise destination would be chosen in accordance with local conditions such as the weather and the availability of water. The state of the pastures was of special concern, since over-grazing could destroy the finely balanced ecology and result in chronic erosion of the soil (as was to happen in many parts of Central Asia in the twentieth century).

Securing pasturage for their flocks was the chief but not sole concern of the nomads. They also required reeds (to make the mat-like inner skin of the tent), various types of wood (for use as fuel, for the manufacture of saddles, looms and other implements, and for the construction of the trellised frame of the tent). The nomads were also skilled hunters, using simple weapons or specially trained falcons and eagles to hunt fur-bearing animals such as wolves, foxes and hares. They engaged in some fishing and in the south, in the winter grounds, in a little agriculture. Each community had its own blacksmiths, carpenters and other craftsmen who could make the common objects of everyday life. More sophisticated implements and luxury goods, as well as staple commodities such as grain, were acquired through trade with the sedentary populations on the periphery of the nomads' territory.

Territorial divisions

The distances covered annually by the nomads varied greatly from region to region. The average length of a day's journey was quite short, usually some 10–15 kilometres. The distance between summer and winter destinations, however, could be 1,000 kilometres or more.[8] The 'Kazakh lands', for the nomads, formed three, discrete 'economic units'. One was in the south, stretching westwards from Lake Balkhash approximately to the channel of the Sarysu river, southwards to the Syr Darya and eastwards into the Altai and Tien Shan mountains. The relief in this region is more varied than in the central sections and the nomads could find different environments within a relatively short range, generally between 200 and 300 kilometres, by moving

---

8 A series of maps published by the Kazakh Academy of Sciences (Alma-Ata, 1980) shows the traditional routes of transhumance, with details of water sources, types of soil and vegetation.

vertically from the sheltered pastures of the river valleys on the plains to the lush green subalpine and alpine meadows of the mountains in the east and southeast. The nomads here were able to interact with the sedentary communities of the Ili and Fergana valleys. This 'unit' was eventually to form the core of the lands of the Kazakh 'Big Horde' (*Ulu zhus*).

A second unit was located in the centre, encompassing the deserts of the eastern littoral of the Aral Sea and extending northwards to the basins of the Tobol, Ishim and Irtysh on the fringes of the Siberian steppe. The migration routes here were the longest, often well over 1,000 km from the winter grounds in the south to the summer grounds in the north. The sedentary population with which this group had economic, and at times cultural and political links, was that of the towns and cities of the oasis belt of the middle reaches of the Syr Darya. This was to become the territory of the Kazakh 'Middle Horde' (*Orta zhus*).

The land lying between the lower course of the Volga and the western margin of the Aral Sea constituted the third 'unit'. Here the annual cycle of transhumance took the nomads from winter grounds in the vicinity of the relatively mild littoral belt of the Caspian Sea to the uplands between the Ural, Irgiz and Turgai rivers. The sedentary population with whom they traded (and whose settlements they sometimes raided) was that of the lower Volga region. The Kazakh 'Little Horde' (*Kishi zhus*) took possession of this territory.

Clans, tribes and hordes

Traditional Kazakh society was characterized by a blend of dependence and independence, subordination and insubordination. The rigidity of the structural hierarchies – born of a long tradition of field warfare – was offset by the inherent mobility of nomad life, a mobility that required not only physical endurance, but also self-reliance and the ability to take personal decisions and responsibility. Thus, despite the very strong bonds of communal obligations and loyalties, ultimately the nomads remained free agents and if dissatisfied could, and not infrequently did, move with their households and flocks to a new location. This flexibility gave the tribal structure a dynamism that enabled it to accommodate the constantly changing shape and balance of regional power politics. It only lost this elasticity when, after annexation and sedentarization, the tribes ceased to have any real function and were reduced to the status of genealogical markers.

Clans and tribes

The basic socio-economic unit in Kazakh nomad society was the encampment (*auyl*). This constituted a 'clan', consisting of an extended patriarchal family network; maternal relatives from other clans (the Kazakhs were rigorously exogamous, with no consanguinity in the male line permitted within seven generations); also freed slaves and others who had attached themselves to the community. Members of the encampment were divided into separate households, each with its own tent. The number of tents in an encampment varied greatly; in the eighteenth century 3–15 was the norm, but many more might congregate around a khan ('supreme ruler'). Several encampments would come together for the long summer migration; they would also unite in time of war or other periods of danger. During the winter, however, they would separate into their original units, to have a better chance of finding good pasturage. Each encampment had its own elected leader, who would make the major decisions concerning the wellbeing of the community. The encampments were loosely grouped into tribal units, whose number varied as a consequence of the process of fragmentation and amalgamation that continued into the early nineteenth century. The names and distinctive attributes (war-cries, insignia) of the main tribes, however, were preserved,[9] and the histories of some have been traced back (albeit speculatively) as far as the eighth century AD or earlier.

The fluidity of nomad allegiances was such that members of the same tribe often came to be divided between different 'hordes', some of which later coalesced into more stable ethnopolitical groupings. Consequently, several of the tribes that were incorporated into the Kazakh Khanate and were subsequently considered to be 'Kazakhs' were also represented in neighbouring states, where they played a similarly formative role; for example, the Naimans are represented not only among the Kazakhs, but also among the Kyrgyz, Karakalpaks, Nogais and Uzbeks.[10] Today these links tend to be emphasized by those who espouse pan-Turkic views, but downplayed by those of a more narrowly nationalist persuasion.

'Aristocrats' and 'commoners'

The tribes were ruled by a dual aristocracy. The sultans or *tore* were 'white bone' nobles, directly descended in the male line from Mongol princes, almost invariably of, or laying claim to be of, the house of Genghiz Khan. Closely related to one another, they were nevertheless frequently involved in internecine power struggles. They

---

9 Tynyshpayev, *Materialy*, pp. 28–9.
10 Tynyshpayev, *Materialy*, pp. 27–8.

did not form part of the clan-tribal system, although they 'possessed' groups of clans or tribes, on whose support they depended in their bids for supremacy within the Khanate. Only they could elect the khan from among their own number, and they ruled by skill and their ability to balance conflicting tribal interests. As eighteenth-century Russian envoys reported, 'The rulers have almost no power over their elders and people ... Their strength lies in the deciphering of the interests and benefits of the people ... and by giving gifts to the elders and the people they sway them to their purposes.'[11] Also regarded as 'white bone' nobles were the *khodzha*, a revered group of Muslim clerics who claimed direct lineal descent from the Arab Sayyids ('Descendants of the Prophet') who had brought Islam to Transoxiana in the eighth century. Like the sultans, they did not form part of the clan-tribal system.

The 'black bone' aristocracy constituted what in theory was an elected ruling elite, but in practice was often hereditary. Unlike the 'white bone' nobles, the 'black bone' belonged to the clan-tribal structure. There were two categories, the *batyr* ('hero') and the *bii* ('interpreter of customary law', 'judge'). The actual function as well as the power of these individuals depended on circumstances and on personal charisma. Some fulfilled both a legal and a military role. Many had jurisdiction over only one or two clans but a few were able to attract a following of substantial numbers of clans and sub-tribes. Such men were as powerful and independent as any 'white bone' sultan; not infrequently they conducted separate negotiations with rulers of neighbouring states, including, eventually, the Russians. The 'black bone' leaders dealt directly with clan-tribal affairs, while at the same time acting as intermediaries for the sultans and khans, who were the titular leaders.

The 'commoners' were subdivided into a number of categories. The largest was that of the *sharua*, clan-tribe members of middling standing, owning around 10 head of cattle per family. The *bai* formed the wealthier stratum, some of them owning several hundred head of cattle and having poorer families as their dependants; it was they who acted as heads of encampments. The poorest clansmen, those without animals of their own, would work as shepherds or domestic servants for others. Slaves were generally acquired as human booty from raids on neighbouring lands.[12]

Hordes

From its inception in the mid-fifteenth century the Kazakh Khanate was riven by internal feuds and power struggles. Although in principle only one ruler at a time could lay claim to the overall leadership of the Khanate, in practice it was not unusual

---

11 V.A. Moiseyev, *Dzhungarskoye Khanstvo XVII-XVIII vv.* (Alma-Ata, Gylym, 1991), p. 89.
12 M. Bizhanov, 'Sotsialnyye kategorii kazakhskogo obshchestva ...' in Suleimenov, *Kazakhstan*, pp. 150–70.

for two or more rival khans to be ruling concurrently. A further complication is that a number of khans commanded a following that cut across conventional tribal-territorial boundaries.[13] At some unrecorded point in the sixteenth century there was a division of the Khanate into three separate 'hordes', each headed by a khan drawn from the ruling 'white bone' elite of the line of Genghiz Khan. Thus the split did not represent a reshaping of the clan-tribal system, but a formalization of the fragmentation of power that had long been endemic. As mentioned above, the physical territories of the new hordes coincided with the long-established patterns of transhumance.

Even after the formation of the three separate hordes, a loose confederative link was maintained, symbolized by 'summit meetings' of the three khans (at first annually, later more irregularly) to discuss, though not necessarily to reach agreement on, matters of common concern; also, from time to time, to elect from among their number a 'supreme khan' whose authority was, however, for the most part nominal. These tenuous vestiges of a shared political genesis apart, the khans of the hordes acted as heads of independent states, pursuing their own interests, in conflict or in alliance with one another, as often as with their 'foreign' neighbours. Occasionally one khan would succeed in uniting all three hordes for a few years, but none succeeded in forging a lasting union.

Nomad religion and culture

Animism and Islam

The religious world of the Kazakh tribes was informed by two sets of beliefs: a substratum of animism onto which was gradually grafted a veneer of Islam. The former had its roots in ancient Turkic and Mongolian tradition. The central focus was the cult of the sky, with its related manifestations of sun, moon, stars, thunder and lightning; earth and water were also revered as deities, while fire was regarded as a purifying force.[14] The spirits of the dead were thought to have the power to protect the living: graves were therefore treated with respect, furnished with as fine and permanent a marker as possible, be it a mausoleum, a pile of stones or a simple wooden pole. Shamanistic rituals were performed by *baqsi*, who were credited with healing and soothsaying abilities. These and other animistic practices and beliefs were not eradicated by Islam. Rather, there was a gradual syncretic fusion of the old and the new.

The rhythm of nomad life, with its constant movement over long distances and lack of a permanent base, was not conducive to a spread of the orthodox, mosque-

---

13 A. Sabrykhanov, 'K istorii zemel'nykh otnoshenii ... v XVIII veke', in Suleimenov, *Kazkhstan*, p. 154.
14 *Istoriya*, I, pp. 103, 187.

centred faith of the sedentary population. The cities of Transoxiana were converted to Islam in the immediate aftermath of the Arab invasion of the seventh to eighth centuries, and within a hundred years or so were already flourishing centres of Muslim learning and culture. The nomadic tribes of the deserts and steppes, however, were drawn to the new religion more slowly. Nevertheless, by the tenth century most of what is now southern and central Kazakhstan had probably converted to Islam, even if only superficially. Subsequently, in the thirteenth to fourteenth centuries, the Mongols of both the Golden Horde and the Ulus of Chagatai (see Chapter 2) became Muslims. Consequently, by the time of the formation of the Kazakh Khanate, both the 'white bone' aristocracy and the bulk of the tribes were Muslim.

Nomad culture

The culture of the nomads was grounded in the skills necessary for the survival of the community, and of the individual within the community. They had no 'fine art': their aesthetic sensibility was expressed through applied and functional arts. Much of their culture was, by its very nature, ephemeral, shaped by a long, in many ways highly sophisticated tradition, but enacted in the present, in response to immediate needs. While the nomad way of life was a living reality there was no need for elaborate explanations and documentation; once exposed to exogenous influences, however, it soon began to disintegrate, leaving in its wake a patchwork of half-remembered, readily misinterpreted, traditions and images.

The material culture of the nomads was characterized by a combination of simplicity of construction and wealth of ornamentation. Common implements were decorated with intricate designs and patterns. The felt-making tradition was especially highly developed.[15] The oral literature was exceptionally rich and varied. The nomads prized verbal adroitness and the apposite use of aphorisms, riddles, proverbs and similes. There was a strong tradition of story-telling, which drew on local sources as well as the 'international' repertory of Chinese, Middle Eastern and Indian themes. Professional bards were respected members of society, no ceremony or solemn occasion being complete without their participation. They improvised their own songs and poems as well as performing from memory set pieces that had been handed down from generation to generation.[16]

---

15 V. Basilov *et al.* (eds), *Nomads of Eurasia* (Seattle, University of Washington Press, 1989), is well illustrated and provides good descriptions of the history and use of objects of material culture.
16 The best study in English of the Kazakh oral tradition is T.G. Winner, *The Oral Art and Literature of the Kazakhs of Russian Central Asia* (Durham NC, Durham University Press, 1958).

One of the most complex areas of nomad culture was the 'etiquette of behaviour'.[17] Every aspect of the relationship between individuals, and likewise between the individual and the community, was regulated by strict convention. There were general precepts concerning, for example, filial respect and hospitality. There were also many specific obligations of duty, loyalty and responsibility. There was a strong sense of group involvement, with responsibility for the payment of a penalty automatically devolving to fellow clan members if the individual concerned was unable to satisfy the requirement.

Every stage of the life-cycle was accompanied by ceremonies and rituals and these, too, were communal events. At all times, however, a hierarchical protocol was observed, clearly articulating the relative status of the participants. This same sense of order and propriety was reflected in many other areas of life, not least in the spatial organization within the yurt, where each sector had a designated function and social ranking, from the lowly station near the door to the place of honour against the far wall. These and other niceties of etiquette underpinned and expanded the verbal level of communication, creating a context in which the rules of conduct were clear to all and could be manipulated to convey particular messages of satisfaction or displeasure.

Shifting interests, shifting alliances

The period from the late seventeenth to the late eighteenth century is, from a modern perspective, one of the most significant chapters in the history of the Kazakhs, since it represents a critical cusp in the evolution of Kazakh nationhood. At the beginning of this period, the Hordes were (given the general instability of the age and the place) relatively well-defined, independent tribe-states; by the end of it, they were weak, fragmented and firmly under the domination of their neighbours. It was a time of change, of a reapportioning of the balance of regional power. Two powerful new contenders for mastery of the steppes emerged: the Dzhungars (a nomadic Mongol people) in the east and the Russians in the west.[18] The Russians had become active players in the politics of the steppe as a result of their conquest of the Tatar strongholds of Kazan (1552) and Astrakhan (1556), which extended Russian territory up to the borders of the lands of the Little Horde.

Popular histories of the Soviet era were wont to depict this three-cornered contest – between the Kazakhs, the Russians and the Dzhungars – in schematic fashion as a heroic struggle between the evil predators in the east, the magnanimous power in the

---

17 Zh.K. Karakuzova, M.Sh. Khasanov, *Kosmos Kazakhskoy kul'tury* (Almaty, Evraziya, 1993), p. 21, use this expression to sum up the complex rules of behaviour in Kazakh society, past and present.
18 Moiseyev, *Dzhungarskoe Khanstro*, p. 43.

west and the hapless victims in the centre who, had they not had the good fortune to secure the protection of the 'right' side, would have been annihilated. More scholarly studies reveal a situation of far greater complexity, with pragmatism and self-interest the predominant motives on all sides. With the benefit of hindsight it is clear that the eventual outcome – namely, Russian domination – was inevitable. However, at the time it was not so obvious: the Kazakh leaders were past masters at exploiting the ambitions of would-be patrons, and in the short term their strategy of playing one off against the other and negotiating with two sides simultaneously appeared to enable them to turn almost any situation to their advantage (a pattern of behaviour not entirely unfamiliar to those attempting to work in Kazakhstan today). In the longer term, however, this was not a sustainable policy. They became ever more dependent on external support and were finally reduced to the status of virtual pawns of their more powerful neighbours.

Dzhungar raids

The Dzhungars had been making raids on Kazakh lands since the middle of the seventeenth century, but it was not until the early eighteenth century that they succeeded in occupying much of the basin of the Syr Darya; in 1724–5 Turkestan (by this time the capital of the Middle Horde) and Tashkent (the capital of the Big Horde) were taken. This was a fearful blow for the Kazakhs, resulting in a major loss of human and animal life. During this period, known in Kazakh history as the 'Great Calamity', trade and agriculture were disrupted and migration routes changed, thereby altering the whole economic structure of the region.[19] There was a significant shift of population towards the north and northwest, away from Transoxiana. In 1728–9 the united forces of the three Kazakh hordes succeeded in inflicting a series of defeats on the Dzhungars, but the alliance was short-lived and the Little and Middle Hordes abandoned the Big Horde, part of which soon again fell under the tutelage of the re-ascendant Dzhungars.

By the late 1740s, however, the Dzhungar Khanate was in decline. It was finally destroyed by the Ching armies in 1756–8. This brought the Chinese empire across the Tien Shan mountains, to border directly on the lands of the Middle Horde and to occupy some of the territory of the Big Horde.

---

19 A. Sabyrkhanov in Suleimenov, *Kazakhstan*, pp. 146–59.

Russian protection

Throughout the period 1680–1760 Russian influence over the Kazakhs increased. It was, however, by no means a smooth, seamless progression. The process began in the late seventeenth century, when individual Kazakh khans and sultans started to apply for Russian assistance or protection, ostensibly against the Dzhungars, but often also in order to strengthen themselves relative to other Kazakh leaders. Equally, the Russian Tsars appreciated the strategic and economic potential of controlling the Kazakh steppes.[20] In the course of the 1730s the khans of all Kazakh hordes made at least nominal acknowledgments of Russian suzerainty, but some factions opposed rapprochement with the Russians. Even those who had taken the oath of allegiance to St Petersburg not infrequently had second thoughts and made commitments to the Dzhungars and the Chinese instead or as well. Ultimately the complex manoevrings and internal divisions served only to weaken the Kazakh hordes and open the door to external pressure and eventual control. By the end of the eighteenth century both the Little and the Middle Hordes were in a state of disintegration, destroyed by internal feuds as much as by the machinations of external sponsors.[21] The Big Horde, then mostly under Chinese rule, was also rapidly unravelling. By the time the Russians finally abolished the office of khan in the Middle Horde in 1822, in the Little Horde in 1824 and in the Bukei Horde (an offshoot of the Little Horde) in 1845, it had long ceased to be of even nominal significance.

Annexation

Territorial expansion

The territorial annexation of Kazakh lands was a somewhat simpler undertaking for the Russians than was securing the loyalty of the Kazakh hordes. As early as 1520 an outpost was founded at Yaitsk (later renamed Ural'sk) on the Ural (Yaik) river, on the western margin of what was subsequently to become the territory of the Little Horde; Gur'yev (now Atyrau), at the mouth of the Ural river, close to the Caspian Sea, was founded in 1645. In the early eighteenth century, as a consequence of Russia's opening up of Siberia, bases were established along the northeastern rim of the Kazakh lands, at Omsk in 1716, Semipalatinsk in 1718 and Ust'-Kamenogorsk in 1720. In

---

20 K. Kereyeva-Kanafiyeva, *Dorevolyutsionnaya russkaya pechat' o Kazakhstane* (Alma-Ata, Kazgosizdat, 1963), p. 23; also B. Ya. Basin, 'Kazakhstan v sisteme vneshney politiki Rossii ...', in Suleimenov, *Kazakhstan*, p. 54.
21 This period is analysed in detail, drawing on archival material, by B. Ya. Basin, in Suleimenov, *Kazakhstan*, pp. 50–145.

1740–50 they were incorporated into a fortified border defence system. The formal granting of protection to the Little Horde was the pretext for creating additional strongholds in the northwest, along the middle course of the Ural river, at Orsk (1735) and at Orenburg (1743). These bases were linked together to form a fortified line, manned by Cossacks, that gave the Russians both military and economic control of southern Siberia as well as of Kazakh lands in the northern steppe.

The Russian domination of the interior was not attempted till the next century, when it was accomplished with extraordinary speed. New settlements appeared in rapid succession, spread out over a huge radius. In 1824 alone, Akmolinsk, Kokchetav and Karkaralinsk were founded. The central steppe-desert zone was secured by fortresses at Raim (Aral'sk), Kazaly (Kazalinsk) and Verny (Almaty), established in 1847–54. Still further to the south, the Russians encountered, and captured with relative ease, the towns and cities of the Syr Darya which, although by this time mostly under the control of the Khans of Kokand, had for the past two centuries constituted the southern margin of the 'Kazakh lands'. Ak-Mechet' (Kzyl-Orda) was taken in 1853, Turkestan, Aulie-Ata (Zhambul) and Chimkent in 1864, Tashkent in 1865.

Although the charters granting imperial protection to the Little and Middle Hordes marked the formal incorporation of these entities (leaving aside the question of who or what these entities were) into the Russian empire, the Russian side of Russo-Kazakh relations continued to be handled by the College of Foreign Affairs, on the same footing as relations with other foreign states; visiting Kazakh dignitaries were likewise known as envoys and ambassadors.[22] It was not until 1782, after Catherine II had pointed out that 'the Horde' was numbered among the subjects of the empire, and that its affairs must therefore be regarded as domestic, that Russo-Kazakh questions were handed over to the jurisdiction of the Procurator General. The Big Horde, however, still mostly under Chinese rule, continued to be considered a foreign state, with relations regulated by the College until 1847.

Opposition

Since the Russian annexation of the Kazakh steppes was prompted, at least nominally, by the request of the khans for imperial protection, there was no opposition movement *per se* against the Tsarist administration in the early period. Nevertheless, there were a number of localized insurrections. Most of these were spontaneous, short-lived incidents, provoked by the limitations imposed by the Russian authorities on the use of traditional grazing grounds. A more serious challenge to a Russian-backed ruling clique occurred in 1836–7; the armed encounters were of no great military consequence but

---

22 Suleimenov, *Kazakhstan*, p. 50.

the conflict and the grievances of the insurrectionists were immortalized in verse and came to be known throughout the Kazakh world. A number of other uprisings followed, mostly small-scale, sometimes instigated and supported by the khans of Khiva and Kokand, sometimes having an overtly Muslim character. The most serious episode of all was the bloody uprising of 1916 which, in the space of a few months, engulfed virtually the entire region. In most areas this was soon crushed, but in Turgai it merged into the 1917 February revolution.[23]

First contacts

Until the massive influxes of Slav immigrants in the late nineteenth and early twentieth centuries the number of Russians in Kazakhstan was comparatively small. Nevertheless, from the mid-eighteenth century onwards they had a profound effect on the economic, cultural and political life of the northern steppes. Inexorably, nomadism began to give way to sedentarization and Europeanization. In the south, the Russian impact was much weaker, partly because this region was incorporated into the empire much later, partly because it was physically so much further away from the Russian border and therefore more difficult to penetrate fully, and partly because of the established influence of the neighbouring sedentary Muslim communities.

Administrative-territorial reforms

By the early nineteenth century the Russians had sufficient control over the Middle and Little Hordes to be able to impose a series of radical administrative reforms. These steadily increased Russian's direct involvement in the management and exploitation of the region and at the same time fatally undermined the geographic, economic and social foundations of the clan-tribal system. They introduced a system of territorially based administrative units, which ostensibly were meant to coincide with traditional clan-tribal groupings, but which in fact, since they did not take account of the patterns of transhumance, cut across these boundaries, thereby disrupting the established system of migration. The sultans and other leading Kazakhs lost their hereditary grazing grounds, but those who were well-disposed towards the Russian government were co-opted into the new administrative apparatus and, in effect, became Russian civil servants.

The last stage in the reapportionment of Kazakh lands, which, after one further administrative reallocation, was to remain in force until the Soviet period, was en-

---

23 A re-evaluation of this uprising is now in progress. It is generally agreed, however, that too little material is available as yet for any firm assessment to be made as to the causes and political significance of the event. See proceedings of 1990 Conference *Natsional'nyye dvizheniya v usloviyakh kolonializma* (Tselinograd, al-Farabi, 1991) pp. 103–16.

acted in 1867–8. The avowed aim of this exercise, as stated in the relevant Provisional Statute, was 'to unite the subject peoples of Russia under one administration, to distance the local aristocracy from power, to weaken clan links, in order to achieve the gradual merging of the Kirghiz steppes with other parts of Russia'.[24] In fact, the redrawing of boundaries which ensued did not unite the Kazakhs within a single administrative entity, but divided them between three separate administrations, each of which was further sub-divided into new provincial units (*oblast'*): the Ural and Turgai *oblast'* came under the jurisdiction of the Governor-General of Orenburg, Akmolinsk and Semipalatinsk under the Governor-General of Western Siberia, and Syr Darya and Semirechiye under the Governor-General of Turkestan (who also had jurisdiction over the recently acquired possessions of the Khanates of Bukhara, Khiva and Kokand).

This new tripartite disposition did not coincide with the old horde boundaries but cut through them, dividing clan-tribal units. Perhaps more importantly, it destroyed the coherence of the ancient 'economic zones' which, with their unique combination of different types of fodder, weather conditions, sources of water, fuel and other resources, had sustained the nomad way of life for hundreds of years. The borders between the regional government territories were not, of course, sealed, but the very fact of having different jurisdictions, with different bureaucracies, made it difficult to move from one area to another. Moreover, the division institutionalized the gulf which had been emerging throughout the century between the industrializing regions of the northern tier, already tightly bound into the Russian economy and possessing a large (and constantly expanding) immigrant population, and the southern tier, which remained within the orbit of the sedentary Muslim population of the Syr Darya belt and was politically engaged, alternately as allies and enemies of the Turkmens, Khivans, Kokandis and Bukharans. Even after the Russian conquest of Transoxiana (1865–75) and Transcaspia (early 1880s), this region retained a very different character from the European-influenced north. Today, a century later, this gulf is still in evidence.

Socio-economic change

The first consequence of increased contacts with the Russians was the impact on the regional economy. The border forts soon became trading centres where Russian merchants could do business not only with the nomads, but also with traders from Khiva, Bukhara and Tashkent. This led to a dramatic development and diversification of trade.[25] In the 1830s regular fairs were established, linked to those in Nizhny Novgorod and other major commercial centres. Russian merchants were primarily interested in the

---

24 *Istoriya*, I, p. 385.
25 Suleimenov, *Kazakhstan*, p. 134.

purchase of horses and sheep. Imports from Russia included metal implements as well as dye-stuffs, china, glassware and grain.[26] Kazakh *bais* – the richer 'commoners' – began to act as middlemen in these exchanges, sometimes amassing a considerable fortune in the process. By this time, almost two-thirds of the trade with Russia was cash-based rather than barter, with the move to a money economy accelerated by the Russian authorities' requirement that the yurt tax (introduced in 1837) be paid in silver coinage.

New industries were also opening up, bringing opportunities for waged work. The salt pans of the centre and northeast began to be exploited commercially, and fishing and hunting were commercialized and oriented towards the needs of the Russian market. Small-scale plants for the primary processing of local products, such as tobacco, were set up.[27] Towards the end of the century there was a major expansion in all sectors of the mining industry. Copper and lead had been mined since the end of the eighteenth century, but with the injection of west European and American capital many more deposits of these, as well as of gold and silver, were exploited. The output of coal in the Karaganda region also rose sharply.[28] Many of the new jobs were taken by immigrants, but by the end of the century several thousand Kazakhs were employed in commercial enterprises of one sort or another, mostly as unskilled seasonal labour. Later, the expansion of the Orenburg-Tashkent railway also provided work for relatively large numbers of Kazakhs.

The move towards a sedentary, or semi-sedentary, way of life was a gradual process, triggered by a combination of factors. The increasing dependency on money was accompanied by a general crisis in the nomad economy. This was provoked primarily by the administrative reforms which resulted in the expropriation of essential grazing grounds, and the disruption of patterns of transhumance, as a consequence of which it became difficult to maintain optimum flock sizes. This, coinciding with a number of devastating cases of zhut, and the ongoing predations of marauders from the south, tipped the always marginal balance of nomad existence towards mass pauperization. The situation was exacerbated by the fragmentation of the old social structure: many of the traditional leaders of society – the sultans, batyrs and biis – opted for collaboration with the Russian administration, had their own ambitions, and were no longer intimately concerned with the welfare of their former clan-tribal dependants. The bais likewise had economic interests outside their immediate community and did not depend exclusively on animal husbandry. By the end of the century nomadic pastoralism was still widespread, especially in the south, but society was already in transition and the trend towards at least partial sedentarization was becoming more pronounced.

26 *Istoriya*, I, pp. 296–7.
27 *Istoriya*, I, p. 426.
28 *Istoriya*, I, p. 424.

Cultural change: beginnings of Europeanization/Russification

As Russia strengthened its economic and administrative grip on Kazakhstan, so, too, did the influence of Russian culture become more pervasive. One channel was through state-sponsored education. The first Russian-medium schools were opened in the second half of the eighteenth and early nineteenth centuries, in Omsk, Orenburg, Petropavlovsk and Yamyshevskaya. They were intended chiefly to serve the needs of the local Russian military and civilian communities, but some also admitted Kazakhs. From 1789, however, institutions of higher education were established with the specific aim of providing a Russian education for the children of the Kazakh aristocracy. The intention was 'to facilitate the rapprochement of Asiatics to Russians, to inspire in the former love and confidence towards the Russian government and to provide the region with educated personnel'.[29] In addition to these 'advanced' establishments, which played a crucial role in the Russification of the Kazakh elite, the regional authorities were required to open mixed Russo-Kazakh primary schools in all the district (*uyezd*) centres. In 1895 there were 38 of these schools; by 1913, 157.[30] Kazakh children were also permitted to attend Russian village schools. As a result of these measures a basic knowledge of Russian, Russian culture and the rudiments of a European-style education were disseminated quite widely, particularly in the north, where there were high concentrations of Russian settlers and hence of Russian schools.

A second channel of Russian cultural influence was through manners, dress, furnishings and popular entertainments. The Kazakh aristocracy developed a liking for French gloves, officers' tunics and epaulettes; they danced – in the European style – at evening receptions and in general modelled their behaviour on that of Russian courtiers. Lower down the social scale, the *sharua* also began to adopt new ways, acquiring hitherto unfamiliar items such as mirrors, samovars, sewing machines, candles (a significant innovation, extending the daily routine beyond sunset), bedsteads and stoves; when the nomads and semi-nomads set off on their summer migration, the heavier objects would be left behind in the winter grounds, in quarters that increasingly were becoming permanent constructions. Music was another area in which there was a notable change; European music was frequently heard in public places and Kazakh musicians began to adapt some of these melodies, thereby creating a new Europeanized musical vocabulary.[31]

The trade fairs encouraged the development of a 'public' culture: skills and crafts were no longer used to satisfy the needs and tastes of a small, familiar, 'private' commu-

---

29 *Istoriya*, I, p. 306.
30 *Istoriya*, I, p. 546.
31 P.V. Aravin, B.G. Erzakovich, *Muzykal'naya Kultura Kazakhstana* (Alma-Ata, Kazgosizdat, 1955), pp. 12–13.

nity, but were directed towards a wider, more complex, audience. A class of professional artisans emerged – blacksmiths, carpenters, rug-makers and the like – whose wares were designed to appeal as much to the Russian market as to the nomads. Traditional pastimes such as story-telling and horse-racing also acquired a more 'packaged', less spontaneous character in the multi-ethnic bustle of the fairs. In time, it was this artificial environment that came to set the norm for popular perceptions of folk culture.

Another source of Russian influence, socially and geographically more limited in outreach, but of profound importance in the development of a European-style cultural environment, was the lively intellectual life of the urban-based immigrant communities. These included doctors, teachers, engineers and other permanently resident professionals, visiting scholars, and thousands of political exiles, not only from Russia, but from other parts of the empire as well (among them Ukrainians and a large contingent of Poles), who represented all the main trends in revolutionary thought from the 1820s onwards.

Throughout the northern tier, these groups organized learned societies devoted to such subjects as music, medicine, oriental studies, agriculture and science. They produced scholarly publications and also received the latest journals, books and newspapers from the metropolis. Local newspapers began to appear in Orenburg, Omsk and Ural'sk in the last quarter of the nineteenth century. Public libraries were set up (by 1913, there were 146 on the territory of present-day Kazakhstan), as well as local museums. Repertory companies from Russia regularly spent a season visiting cities such as Orenburg, Petropavlovsk, Pavlodar and Semipalatinsk. A permanent Russian theatre company was established in Orenburg in 1858.[32] Thus, despite their physical remoteness from Russia, the settlements in northern Kazakhstan were by no means intellectual backwaters. The Russian-educated Kazakh elite, numerically very small and still very shallowly grounded, had close ties with these immigrant communities, underpinned in several cases by strong personal friendships. Such links were of inestimable value in broadening the horizons of these young Kazakhs, giving them direct access to the works, and sometimes the persons, of the leading Russian thinkers of the day.

A fourth way in which Russian culture played a definitive role in the transformation of Kazakh society was through its function as recorder, classifier and interpreter of the nomad legacy. Like an Egyptian mummy suddenly exposed to the air, this way of life began to disintegrate as soon as it came into contact with the Russian state. It would have disappeared almost without trace had it not been for the efforts of Russian or, later, Russian-trained Kazakh, scholars to capture in writing and in line drawings, in museums, on film and eventually on magnetic tape, whatever could be transfixed in time. The work of these painstaking observers is of enormous importance and all the

---

32 *Istoriya*, I, p. 478.

more valuable in that it stretches over a period of well over a hundred years, compiled by people of different educational backgrounds, professions and political views. Inevitably, however, it was a record seen through alien eyes, using perspectives and analytical paradigms that were not always appropriate.

Religion

Under the Tsarist administration it was not only Russian influence that was increased. The authorities encouraged Tatars from the Volga region to proselytize Islam among the Kazakh nomads, presumably on the grounds that any 'religion of the book' would exert a civilizing influence, especially when propagated by those who had already been part of the Russian empire for over two centuries. In 1788 a Muftiat was established at Orenburg, thereby facilitating the activities of the Tatar missionaries. State funds were made available for the construction of mosques and the printing of Muslim literature. Although the Tatars were, like the Kazakhs (at least superficially), Sunni Muslims of the Hanafi school, they were at first much resented by the latter: traditionally, mullas had come from the south, from such cities as Turkestan and Tashkent. The Tatar mullas were not only strangers, they were also intent on inculcating more orthodox practices and beliefs; moreover, they requisitioned valuable land for the building of mosques. Gradually, however, they came to be more accepted and succeeded in raising Islamic consciousness; by the turn of the century this had become one of the chief 'boundary markers' between the Kazakhs and the immigrant Slavs.

By the second half of the nineteenth century the Russians were no longer so sanguine about the spread of Islam and tried to combat it with a campaign to convert the Kazakhs to Christianity. This met with little success. Measures were also introduced to restrict the number of mullas. Mosques and Muslim schools could henceforth be opened only if officially sanctioned; the giving of *vaqf* ('charitable endowments') and collection of obligatory religious taxes was prohibited. Nevertheless, the number of religious educational establishments continued to grow rapidly: in 1895 there were only 31 *mekteb* ('primary schools'); by 1913 there were 267.[33] *Madrasse* ('secondary schools or colleges') existed also in most of the big cities. There is no reliable information concerning Sufi activities at this period, although Soviet and post-Soviet commentators have suggested that individual sufi masters (*ishan*) had bands of devotees (*murid*) numbering between 500 and 1,000 members. No indication is provided as to the beliefs and practices espoused by such groups, hence it is not possible to judge whether they were loose associations that served a primarily social function, or whether they were related to established Sufi orders such as the Naqshbandi, Yasawi or Qadiri.

---

33 *Istoriya*, I, p. 546.

Literacy

The level of literacy amongst the nomads remained very low, but among the sedentary population it was beginning to rise significantly by this time, both in Russian and in Kazakh. There had long been some literature in Kazakh, written in the Arabic script and mostly of a religious nature. During the nineteenth century some 70–80 books appeared; from 1900 onwards, however, there was an explosion of printed works in Kazakh, produced in local cities as well as in St Petersburg, Kazan', Ufa, Tashkent and other Muslim centres. In the years 1900–17 over 200 books were published; a 'significant number' were still on Islamic topics,[34] but there were also works on some secular themes, as well as transcriptions of some of the heroic epics and other examples of oral literature. The first Kazakh-language newspaper began to appear in 1888; a number of other papers appeared after 1905, though none of them survived beyond a few issues, mainly for political reasons.[35]

Political stirrings

The colonial experience provided the impetus for the shift from tribal to national consciousness. To some extent national consolidation was fostered by the practical workings of the administration, which passed decrees and administered laws that affected the population of the region as a whole (or at least, as much of it as was under the control of the Russian state). Maps, ethnographic studies and other scholarly projects also helped to define both the territory and the people. It was, however, the Kazakh 'mobilizers' – the cultural and political activists – who gave substance to the concept of a national identity that transcended horde-tribe boundaries: by delineating a common past, they posited a common future. The reading population was still small, but the introduction of literacy marked a qualitative change in society. It broadened horizons, shifting the focus of concern from the *auyl* to the wider 'imagined' community of the Kazakh-speaking nation. Between the mid-1850s and the establishment of Soviet rule some 70 years later, four political trends may be discerned.

'Enlighteners'

The earliest of these trends was drawn from the first generation of Kazakhs to undergo a Russian education. Deeply impressed by this experience, as also by their wider contacts with the Russian intelligentsia, they regarded the union with Russia as

---

34 *Istoriya*, I, pp. 555–6.
35 M.S. Burabayev, O.A. Segizbayev, *Ideinyye svyazi obschestvenno-filosofskoy mysli Kazakhstana i Rossii* (Alma-Ata, Nauka, 1987), pp. 172–4.

a positive step. They believed that the Kazakhs needed to learn Russian in order to have access to a modern, European-style education. Kazakhs of this groups were convinced of the bankruptcy of the old clan-tribal system, as well as the shortcomings of the Tsarist colonial administration. Their attitude towards Islam was highly critical, often accompanied by a perceptible streak of hostility towards Tatar missionaries. They did, however, admire what they regarded as 'pure', uncontaminated Kazakh traditions.

There were three outstanding proponents of the school of thought, known, during the Soviet period, as 'enlighteners'. The first was Shokan Valikhanov (1835–65), who in many ways epitomized the changes that were taking place in the upper stratum of Kazakh society. A sultan of the 'white bone' aristocracy and kinsman of one of those who had led an uprising against Russian rule in 1822, he attended a Muslim primary school, then entered the Omsk Military Academy; shortly after graduation he was appointed Adjutant to the Governor-General of Western Siberia. During this period he became acquainted with Dostoevsky, who was then in exile in Semipalatinsk. He spent 1859–61 in St Petersburg, where he met several of the leading liberals, read the works of reformist writers such as Chernyshevsky and Dobrolyubov and, as he put it himself, drank in 'European spiritual culture'. Valikhanov produced numerous scholarly works on the history and culture of the Kazakhs, as well as writing about issues of current importance, such as the reform of the Kazakh legal system.[36]

The second member of this trio was Ibrai Altynsaryn (1841–89). Grandson of a famous bii, he was one of the first students at the Orenburg school (1850–57). He was eventually appointed inspector of schools in the Turgai province and pioneered the development of mother-tongue education for Kazakh children. However, despite his championship of Kazakh-language education, Altynsaryn remained convinced that Kazakhs also needed to have a good command of Russian, 'the language of culture and knowledge'.[37]

The third member was Abai Kunanbayev (1845–1904), a prolific and highly gifted poet, prose writer and musician, generally regarded as the founder of modern Kazakh literature. The son of a clan-tribal chief of the Semipalatinsk province, he underwent an extraordinarily broad education: from earliest childhood he was steeped in Kazakh oral culture; a period at a *madrasse* in Semipalatinsk gave him a thorough grounding in classical Arabic, Persian and Chagatai literature; later, having acquired a good knowledge of Russian, he became acquainted not only with Russian literature, but, through

---

36 Sh. Valikhanov's collected works (*Sobraniye sochinenii*, 5 vols, Alma-Ata, Kazsovents, 1985) bear witness to his scholarship, as well as to his wide range of interests.
37 I. Altynsaryn compiled the first Russian reader for Kazakhs, using the Cyrillic script instead of the Arabic for the Kazakh text (*Kirgizskaya khrestomatiya*, Orenburg, 1878).

Russian, with contemporary west European thought and with the works of classical Greek and Roman philosophers; through his friendship with young exiles in Semipalatinsk he was also exposed to the main trends in the Russian political arena. His own work reflected these various influences. He introduced new philosophical ideas into Kazakh literature, as well as new genres, expanding the functional potential of the language. Like Valikhanov and Altynsaryn, Kunanbayev recognized the need for Kazakhs to become acquainted with Russian language and culture since 'Russian science and culture are the key to making sense of the world and the acquisition of this could greatly ease the life of our people'.[38]

'Conservatives'

A great deal is known about the life and works of the three 'enlighteners', partly through their own very extensive (and extremely accomplished) writings; partly because they had many Russian friends and admirers; and in very great measure because, during the Soviet period, they were regarded as proto-Marxian icons and hence became the focus of popular as well as scholarly adulation. By contrast, very little is known about the group of bards, loosely termed the *Zar zaman* ('Bad Times') poets, who were antagonistic to Russian rule and who rejected Russian culture, regarding it as the root cause of the eponymous 'Bad Times'. They espoused orthodox Islamic beliefs and traditional social and moral values. For them, the era of the strong khans was a golden age, free of the corruption and exploitation of the colonial period.

In the late nineteenth and early twentieth centuries their work seems to have been quite widely known and some of it appeared in print. Under Soviet rule, however, they were written out of the national myth and mentioned only in passing (though eventually with some grudging acknowledgment of their artistic merit) in specialist studies.[39]

'Bourgeois nationalists'

Another group about which relatively little is known is that which was labelled 'bourgeois nationalist' by Soviet writers. For the first wave of 'enlighteners', Russian culture had been a revelation, the key to progress, prosperity and social justice. Fifty

---

38 The Soviet Kazakh writer M. Auezov wrote a much acclaimed two-volume biography of Abai, in which he delineated the Kazakh writer's spiritual and philosophical links with democratic Russian literary figures of the time. For an assessment of Abai's socio-political significance, see Burabayev and Segizbayev, *Ideinyye svyazi* ..., pp. 122–57.
39 *Istoriya*, I, pp. 459–61.

years later, the young Kazakh doctors, teachers, engineers, writers and poets of the early twentieth century, although still relatively few in number, were yet numerous and well established enough no longer to feel overawed by the novelty of the European world. Rather, having assimilated what they deemed to be useful, they were becoming self-confident enough to redefine their own identity, albeit within the social, cultural and political framework of the Russian empire.

An important element in this process was the reaffirmation – or more accurately, the elevation – of Islam as a defining feature of Kazakh identity. This found concrete expression in a move to demand that the official administrative designation of the Kazakhs be altered from 'Kirghiz' to 'Muslim Kirghiz'.[40] It fizzled out without achieving its specific goal, but it did highlight the growing significance of Islam as a political force. There is, however, no indication that there was a similar rise of a politicized Islamic awareness among the nomads, who still constituted the majority of the Kazakh population.

There were two other strands in this (urban) Kazakh renaissance. First, there was an upsurge of interest in Kazakh clan-tribal history, directed not so much towards an analysis of its social and political mechanisms (as had been the case in the nineteenth century) as towards a clarification of lineage and genetic roots. An idealized, static representation of the Hordes and their constituent tribal elements was propagated by nationalistically inclined intellectuals. Their work became the basis for subsequent clan-tribal definitions during the Soviet and post-Soviet periods. Secondly, there was a new awareness of a common Turkic heritage that reached beyond the physical and cultural confines of Central Asia to link the Kazakhs not only to the Tatars and other Turkic peoples of the Russian empire, but also to the Turks of the still powerful Ottoman empire. This sense of common identity was strengthened by the fact that quite a number of young Kazakhs were now travelling outside their own region to study in Tatar cities such as Ufa and Kazan, and also in Istanbul.

It is impossible at this stage, given the paucity of documentary evidence from the period, to know how strong this 'bourgeois nationalist' movement was. Soviet writers defined it in terms of a class phenomenon and, notwithstanding its importance, that is very likely to have been the case, since it appears to have appealed principally to the urban-based, relatively affluent Kazakh intelligentsia. Its leaders were broadly in sympathy with the ideas of the Russian 'Kadets' (Constitutional Democrats). They formed the Alash movement, a moderate nationalist grouping, in 1905. During the First World War they remained loyal to the Tsarist government and were opposed to the 1916 insurrection. After the February Revolution, some members of this group formed the

---

40 *Istoriya*, I, pp. 499–500.

anti-Bolshevik Alash Orda government in Orenburg, which survived from late 1917 to 1920. A few were involved in the abortive attempt to establish an autonomous government in Kokand in 1917.[41]

Socialists

The fourth trend was the embryonic socialist movement. Although predominantly Russian, by the early twentieth century it had some support amongst the Kazakhs in the main cities, mines and railheads such as Perovsk (Kzyl Orda), Turkestan, Semipalatinsk and Verny (Almaty). Marxist literature began to penetrate the region in increasing quantities and revolutionaries such as M. V. Frunze (a student in Verny), V. V. Kuibyshev (born in Omsk) and S. M. Kirov embarked on political agitation in the industrial centres of the north. There was already widespread discontent among the Kazakhs, who had seen much of their best land confiscated for reallocation to immigrant Slav settlers and foreign mining companies. The situation was exacerbated by the poor harvest of 1912, which resulted in mass starvation and the outbreak of devastating epidemics. The final blow was the imposition of heavier taxes and service obligations, and the requisitioning of essential supplies, in order to support the Russian war effort: thousands of young Kazakhs were drafted into non-combatant units, many sent to distant parts of the empire, depriving their families of vital manpower resources.[42]

Some sixteen Marxist cells were active in various cities in Kazakhstan in the period 1894–1906.[43] A group of writers and poets emerged who were more radical in their political views than the Alash members, being influenced more by Russian revolutionaries than by Russian liberals. They were generally from a less affluent background, although, like other Kazakh intellectuals of the day, they often combined a Muslim *madrasse* education with some training in Russian.

---

41 For a survey of the views of Muslim political activists in the Russian empire 1917–20, amongst whom were a number of leading Kazakhs, see the collection of original documents reproduced in *Programnye dokumenty musul'manskikh politicheskikh partii 1917–1920 gg.* (Oxford, Society for Central Asian Studies, 1985).
42 M. Auezov *et al.* (eds), *Istoriya Kazakhskoy SSR (Qazaq SSR Tarikhy)*, II, Alma-Ata, ANKazSSR, 1959) (hereafter, *Istoriya*, II), p. 18, estimates that 160,000 Kazakhs were mobilized for such work. They began to return home in the summer of 1917.
43 *Istoriya*, I, pp. 551-3; also the reprint *Kazakhi o russkikh do 1917 goda* (Oxford, Society for Central Asian Studies, 1985), p. 11.

4 SOVIETIZATION

Soviet rule was the definitive experience for the formation of the modern Kazakh identity. It was responsible not only for the radical transformation of contemporary society, but also for the comprehensive reinterpretation of the past – the cultural legacy as well as the historical chronicle – in accordance with the determinist philosophy of Marxism-Leninism. It was during this period that the inchoate sense of Kazakh nationhood that had surfaced in the nineteenth century was selectively expanded and elaborated to provide the basis for a national narrative that traced the 'inevitable' (not to mention 'positive') evolution of the Kazakhs from an amorphous collection of tribes into a fully-fledged Soviet people.

Soviet 'nationality policies' were rooted in the Marxist-Leninist theory of the nation. It was necessary to establish at least the semblance of independent nationhood among the titular peoples of the Soviet republics in order to give credence, however superficially, to the notion that the Soviet state constituted a voluntary union of free nations, and thus was qualitatively different from colonial empires. This resulted in a policy of dual emphasis – of identification with the Soviet state and with the national group – which was to shape the cultural, political and economic life of all the Soviet peoples. However, the impact was strongest in Central Asia, since there it formed part of an intensive modernization campaign. The Kazakhs, still at a comparatively early stage in the transition from a traditional existence (i.e. nomadic pastoralism and an orally transmitted culture) to sedentarization and literacy, were especially vulnerable to Soviet ethnic engineering. The boundaries – physical, metaphorical and imaginary – that were staked out at this time to differentiate the Kazakhs from their neighbours, thereby to give sharper articulation to the formulaic Marxist-Leninist concept of national identity, were thoroughly internalized; consequently, they acquired an emotional validation that largely outweighed traditional ties and even objective historical realities. Thus, the parameters of modern Kazakh nationhood which were established and consolidated over the ensuing seventy-odd years, and which continue to exist today, were essentially a Soviet creation.

Before turning to certain specific aspects of the process of Sovietization in Kazakhstan, there are some general characteristics which must be borne in mind. First, these developments took place within the context of a totalitarian state: therefore, not only were the necessary human and material resources mobilized as and when required, but a unanimity of purpose was achieved through the exercise of the tools of mass manipulation – namely, regimentation, censorship, persuasion and terror. Secondly, despite the immense hardships and anguish of the early years, there emerged in time a genuine sense of optimism, of pride in the heroic struggle to build socialism. Thirdly, there were no sources of information, no points of reference, other than those sanctioned by the state. Fourthly, those who were categorically opposed to the new order took the age-old nomad option of flight, moving in their thousands, with families, tents and flocks, across the still open borders into China, Mongolia, Afghanistan and Iran. These factors, in combination, created an atmosphere in which it was possible to achieve a degree of change which, under any other conditions, would have been inconceivable.

Creating the Soviet Kazakh nation

Demarcation of territorial boundaries

According to Marxist-Leninist theory, one of the key attributes of a nation is a common territory. This, at the time of the 1917 revolution, the Kazakhs did not possess. The situation was partly remedied in 1919 when a preliminary delimitation of the Kazakh lands was carried out, as a result of which the northern provinces of Ural'sk, Turgai, Akmolinsk and Semipalatinsk, the city of Orenburg (which was chosen as the capital of the new formation) and its environs, and also the areas of Astrakhan that were heavily populated by Kazakhs, were united to form the 'Kirghiz (still, at this period, the official designation of the Kazakhs) Territory'. In August 1920 this unit, with the addition of the Kazakh-populated areas of Transcaspia, but still without the southern Kazakh provinces of Turkestan, was transformed into the 'Kirghiz Autonomous Soviet Socialist Republic' (KASSR), within the jurisdiction of the Russian Soviet Federative Socialist Republic (RSFSR). By no means all Kazakhs were in favour of this move to unite huge expanses of territory that already had very mixed populations and different levels of development; even some Kazakh Communists argued in print that the scheme was premature and that there were more urgent matters to be addressed (notably the restoration of basic guarantees of law and order).[44] There were various proposals which sought to maintain the territorial integrity of the region as a whole, through the creation of either a Central Asian federation or a Turkic republic.

---

44 *Istoriya*, II, p. 156.

Nevertheless, the central authorities continued to press for a territorial division along ethnic lines and in 1924–5 the formal National Delimitation of Central Asia was accomplished, whereby the borders of the five main administrative-territorial units (Kazakhstan, Kyrgyzstan, Tajikistan, Turkmenistan and Uzbekistan) were marked out; it is these borders, which in places were slightly modified over the next few decades, that have now become the international frontiers of the post-Soviet independent states of Central Asia. At the time, although the division occurred within the framework of the Soviet Union, and the borders were thus internal, there were bitter disputes between the various nationalist factions as to which areas should be included within their territorial jurisdiction and which allocated to their 'fraternal co-Unionists'. The Kazakhs and the Uzbeks both laid claim to the ethnically mixed Syr Darya region, including Tashkent, and to Karakalpakia.[45] The former acquired most of the Syr Darya region, excluding the city of Tashkent, but including part of the Samarkand region; they were also allocated a swathe of land to the east, up to the Chinese border (formerly part of the territory of the Big Horde), and jurisdiction over Karakalpakia, thus encircling the Aral Sea. In return for these territorial gains in the south, which amounted to some 700,000 square kilometres (almost one and a half times the area of France), the Kazakhs lost Orenburg and its environs. Consequently, the capital of the KASSR, originally located at Orenburg, had to be moved. Ak-Mechet' (later renamed Kzyl-Orda), in the newly acquired southern belt, was chosen as the new seat of government; in 1929 the capital was again moved, this time to the far east, to Alma-Ata (today Almaty), a small town with, at that date, a predominantly Russian population of under 50,000. Boundary changes included in 1932 the loss of jurisdiction over Karakalpakia (which was subsequently attached to Uzbekistan) and in 1963 the reallocation of part of the Hungry Steppe to Uzbekistan. In 1925 the 'Kirghiz' ASSR was officially renamed the 'Kazak' ASSR; in 1936 this was emended to 'Kazakh', in order to reflect more closely Kazakh pronunciation. That same year, in accordance with the provisions of the new Constitution of the USSR, the Kazakh ASSR was elevated to full Union republic status, which it retained until December 1991.

Demarcation of cultural and linguistic boundaries

Three other criteria had to be fulfilled in order to qualify, in Marxist-Leninist terms, for definition as a nation: 'a common language, ... a common economic life, and a common psychological make-up manifested in common specific features of national culture'.[46] The development of a common economic life among the Kazakhs falls

---

45 A.A. Gordienko, *Sozdaniye sovetskoy natsional'noy gosudarstvennosti v Sredney Azii* (Moscow, Gosyurizdat, 1959), p. 168.
46 G. Starushenko, *The Principle of National Self-Determination in Soviet Foreign Policy* (Moscow, Foreign Languages Publishing House, n.d.), p. 22.

outside the scope of this paper, but the issues of language and culture are very relevant to a discussion of the formation of the modern Kazakh identity.

Under Soviet rule, great importance was accorded to the creation of fully functional national languages, both for symbolic reasons (as part of the national development policies) and for the purely practical purposes of mass communication, which, by extension, included mass political indoctrination. Kazakh, unlike most of the other Central Asian languages of the early twentieth century, was relatively well equipped to face these new demands. It had little dialectal variation, hence could already be considered to constitute a unified national language (unlike, for example, Uzbek, which had very marked regional differences). It did not have a very long history as a written medium, but the burst of literary activity during the Tsarist period had served to broaden its functional base and to introduce a modern political and technical vocabulary. Consequently, it was possible to expand the use of the language in public life quite rapidly. As early as November 1923 a decree was passed in the KASSR requiring that official documents be written in Kazakh; similar measures were introduced in the Kazakh-populated districts that were not yet included within the boundaries of the KASSR.[47] In the Kazakh Constitution of 1924 Russian and Kazakh were jointly accorded the status of state languages.

Over the next few decades the vocabulary and phraseology of Kazakh were developed in accordance with the new needs of society; in some fields (e.g. politics, economics, science and technology) this entailed the assimilation of large numbers of Russian/international words. There were also two changes of script: from the Arabic to the Latin in 1929, then from the Latin to the Cyrillic in 1940. The volume of book and periodical publications rose sharply. By 1940, there were 762 book titles published in Kazakhstan (382 in Kazakh), and 13 periodicals and 438 newspapers in Kazakh, with a joint annual print run of almost 77 million copies.[48] Thus the language, in printed and spoken form, was firmly established as a symbol of national identity. This, in conformity with the basic thrust of all Soviet nationality policies, functioned at two levels: on one, the use of a common script (i.e. Cyrillic) and a common terminological fund underlined the supranational Soviet linkage; on the other, the codification of the language, as well as the specific adaptations of the script that were introduced in order to reflect Kazakh pronunciation more effectively, clearly demarcated the national boundaries, differentiating linguistically not only between Russians and Kazakhs, but also between Kazakhs and their Central Asian Turkic neighbours.

If the language could be fitted with comparative ease into the requisite Soviet-style national mould, the same could not be said of Kazakh culture. This was too alien

47 K. Beisembiev, *Pobeda marksistsko-leninskoy ideologii v Kazakhstane* (Alma-Ata, 1970), pp. 22–32, gives an overview of developments during this period.
48 The statistical handbook *Narodnoye khozyaystvo Kazakhstana za 70 let* (Alma-Ata, 1990), p. 112.

and too particular to be assimilated into the Soviet system without major modifications. It was therefore subjected to an intensive process of cultural colonization which, under the guise of modernization, resulted in the wholesale Europeanization/ Russification of Kazakh life. Every sphere of activity was affected, from patterns of socialization to intellectual preoccupations, from table manners to sport. The shift from native to imported customs was inevitably gradual and uneven, more pronounced in some areas than in others. Yet in time it permeated the whole of society, bringing about a decisive change in the Kazakh population's aspirations, self-perceptions and sense of identity.

This transformation was vividly charted in the arts. The guiding dictum of the day for literature, as for all other artistic genres, was that it should be 'national in form, proletarian in content'.[49] In the Kazakh case, however, as elsewhere in Central Asia, the very forms were foreign transplants, born of a different culture and imported to serve in the ideological fight to refashion society. The process had already been set in motion during the Tsarist period, but in a tentative and very limited manner. Kazakh writers, for example, had begun to experiment with European/Russian literary genres in the early twentieth century, but then this was merely one strand in a varied, pluralistic cultural environment. During the Soviet period, by contrast, from the 1920s onwards, European/Russian models became the norm, compulsory exemplars for a rash of imitative novels, short stories, poems and plays. Subsequently, in the 1930s, European/Russian-style Kazakh orchestral and choral music, opera and ballet were developed. In the visual arts, Kazakh painters began to produce landscapes and portraits in the European/Russian tradition; later, graphic art and sculpture in the round also made an appearance.

The subject matter of such works reflected current political priorities, as, for example, the industrialization of the country, the mechanization of agriculture, the construction of railways, class warfare and the fight for gender equality. Analogous operas, ballets, novels and the like were produced in every language and republic of the Soviet Union: the only 'national' features to be found in these creations were the location and the judicious touches of local folklore and historical background (though such elements had to be treated with care in order to avoid the dangerous charge of 'idealizing the past'). These works fulfilled important ideological functions. First, by their very similarity, they gave substance to the idea of a shared Soviet culture; secondly, they reflected diversity within that unity, symbolically emphasizing the boundaries of national identity within the framework of the broader Soviet identity; thirdly, in the 'developing' societies of Central Asia, they provided a ready and impressive

---

49 A. Kanapin, *Kul'turnoye stroitel'stvo v Kazakhstane* (Alma-Ata, 1964), pp. 168–90.

replacement for 'primitive' traditional art. Finally, but by no means of least importance, they furnished the images and interpretations that shaped people's understanding of their history and culture, fleshed out the myths of school textbooks, projected clear, unambiguous ideological messages about present achievements and future goals. These creations were not 'high style' art reserved for a select section of the public, but were integrated into the life of the community through such activities as regular group outings to galleries, theatres and concert halls, and through the systematic study of the new literature at school and university. Thus, in a very direct way, they helped to mediate the new, Soviet-national identities.

Alongside these modern (i.e. European/Russian) art forms, some aspects of 'folk' art were preserved. The reasons for their survival were largely pragmatic. Traditional bards were coopted into the service of the new regime. They composed eulogies in the traditional style on the life and work of Lenin, the achievements of the revolution, the horrors of the past, the bright future that lay ahead and other such politically correct themes. They acted as semi-official cultural ambassadors, performing at state functions and festivals of republican art, and sometimes travelling abroad to participate in similar events in other countries. Skilled craftsmen such as carpet-makers and woodcarvers also continued to produce work in the traditional style, but this was likewise used to serve political ends, their creations being reserved mainly for presentation as gifts to high-ranking visitors or for display in international exhibitions. Some attempt was made to maintain and develop traditional skills, especially with regard to vocal and instrumental music, but the training that was provided in the state-run institutes was heavily influenced by European/Russian norms and lacked the organic link with society that had characterized such activities in the past.

In the face of these constraints, it is not surprising that traditional art forms were soon reduced to the status of cultural tokenism. It is a gauge both of how sterile they had become and of how successful the Kazakhs were in assimilating the new art forms that the creative energy of the younger generation found more stimulating outlets in the latter direction than in the former. After a couple of decades of distinctly derivative work, Kazakh artists began to make strong original contributions in all the main European/Russian artistic genres, both as composers and as performers. A number of them were acclaimed at all-Union level and a few, such as the ballerina Altynai Assylmuratova, became international stars.[50] Given this level of excellence, questions as to whether or not ballet (or any of the other arts acquired during the Soviet era) should be considered an 'authentic' vehicle for Kazakh inspiration are surely

---

50 Since the late 1980s the Alma-Ata-born Altynai Assylmuratova has been dancing leading roles with the Royal Ballet, London, and with other major ballet companies in Western Europe.

irrelevant: by sheer mastery of the medium the Kazakhs made it their own. This pattern of acquisition and internalization was not an exception but rather the rule, contributing to a major cultural shift throughout society.

Implementation 1: Building the new

Since the state had absolute control of all the resources of coercion, reward, and mass communication, there were no systemic obstacles to the implementation of Soviet ideology. In the mid-1920s coordinated assaults were launched on a number of fronts simultaneously. One of the first priorities was the introduction of major programmes of economic and social reform (e.g. reorganization of land ownership; mechanization of agriculture; industrialization; development of transport and communications networks; health care; education; female emancipation; and the reform of family law). These were initiated throughout the Soviet Union. In Kazakhstan, however, as elsewhere in Central Asia, the task was greater since the initial starting point was very much lower. Massive support was provided by the central government in order to transform Central Asian society in such a way as to make possible the integration of the region into the Union and thereby to harmonize policies in all parts of the country. The outcome of these campaigns of accelerated development was the raising of standards of living in Kazakhstan and the other Central Asian republics to a level which, if not quite that of the western republics, was nevertheless well above that of neighbouring Asian countries and far higher than in pre-Soviet Central Asia.

Another priority was institution-building and, as a complement to this, nation-building. Again, this was a Union-wide exercise, but in Kazakhstan and the other Central Asian republics the social and cultural effects were more obvious since the traditional way of life in these areas was very different. Measures that were introduced at this time included the building up of regional branches of the Communist Party and related organizations; the establishment of professional/trade unions; the training of local administrative personnel; and the selection of republican emblems and other distinctive symbols (e.g. flags, anthems, badges). As in other fields, the dual-level hierarchy of Soviet and national identity was carefully articulated. Thus, for example, the Communist Party of Kazakhstan (founded in 1937, on the basis of earlier, regional organizations) was affiliated and subordinated to the Communist Party of the Soviet Union. Similarly, the Kazakh national flag was a modified version of the Soviet flag.

There were many specific strategies that were employed to further the nation-building project. The one that was of crucial significance for the transformation of Kazakh society was the campaign for mass literacy and education. The average level of literacy among the Kazakhs in 1926 was just over 7 per cent. By the early 1930s, adult literacy had risen to an estimated 40 per cent, by 1939 to 77 per cent (85 per cent among the male population).[51] The goal of full adult literacy was achieved in the early 1940s. Meanwhile, the network of schools and other educational facilities was being rapidly expanded. In 1930/31 schooling (which was free) was made compulsory for boys and girls of eight years and above. Boarding facilities were established in order to cater for the needs of nomad children and those who lived in remote rural areas. Higher education was also developed. The Kazakh State University (founded in 1934) had over 3,600 students by 1958, of whom approximately 1,600 were Kazakhs (including 548 Kazakh girls).[52] The Kazakh Academy of Sciences was established in 1946. Academic standards in these institutions came to be acknowledged as amongst the highest in the Soviet Union.

This dramatic shift – from an orally transmitted culture to literacy and book-learning – brought about a fundamental change in the Kazakhs' outlook. Within scarcely more than a generation, a people whose world had formerly been bounded by the limits of personal experience suddenly found their horizons infinitely expanded. Knowledge was no longer strictly related to the struggle for survival: it now served to make sense of a larger, more complex society. As Lenin had anticipated, one important aspect of literacy was that it facilitated the process of political indoctrination, since it opened up many more channels through which ideological propaganda could be disseminated to the population. Another was that it heightened a sense of national identity since, as terms of reference widened, so, too, it became both possible and necessary to locate the community in a broader spatial and chronological framework. At school, legend was replaced by 'proper' scholarly histories, furnished with the confidence-inspiring paraphernalia of dates, statistics and references; maps traced precise contours and specific geographic features: 'Kazakhstan' took on a concrete shape, 'our' territory clearly distinguished from that of 'the others', neighbours far and near; likewise, 'our' history and 'our' heritage, as opposed to 'theirs', was marked out in precise detail, from earliest prehistory to modern times. This process of national definition was further strengthened by the fact that it was not happening in isolation: identical nation-building projects were being undertaken contemporaneously in all the Soviet republics, using the same patterns and the same instruments. In Central Asia, the delimitation of the Kazakh national property was mirrored by a matching process in the adjacent republics of Uzbekistan, Turkmenistan and Kyrgyzstan. Yet as with the establishment of fixed territorial boundaries, a number of areas of disputed possession were created, with more than one of the Central Asian peoples laying exclusive national claim to the same heroes

---

51 *Istoriya*, II, p. 426.
52 *Istoriya*, II, p. 661.

or cultural monuments; potential sources of tension were thus increased rather than diminished by this nation-building exercise, since conflicting claims were institutionalized and thereby imbued with 'objective' respectability.

Two other strategies should be mentioned as an indication of quite how all-embracing was the project of 'cultural construction'. One was the wide-ranging programme of popular, non-formal education. The network of museums and public libraries was vastly extended, the sparsely populated regions of the centre and south being served by mobile units. Party activists organized discussion groups at which books and newspapers were read aloud. Regular talks were provided on a variety of subjects, from art, music and local history to Marxist-Leninist aesthetics, international affairs and the decisions of the Party.[53] Radio, and later television and cinema, played an important part in these outreach activities. Films, both documentary and feature, were extremely popular. A huge infrastructure was developed to service this form of communication: projectors were dispatched to distant settlements, maintenance workers were trained, storage centres for films constructed and rotas established for the loan of reels. By 1958, two to three films a year were being produced in Kazakhstan.[54] Most of these were in Kazakh; those made elsewhere, including a few foreign films, were usually dubbed into Kazakh. A significant proportion of the films carried a strong ideological message, reifying the teachings of the Party and forging a sense of community and common purpose. The distant Soviet capital and the almost equally remote republican capital were integrated into the familiar topography of the most isolated rural outpost; equally, the Soviet as well as the republican leadership became known figures throughout the region.

The second strategy was the use of urbanization. This had two aspects. One was the built environment itself. The Kazakhs, coming from a nomad culture, had no architectural tradition of their own, hence the psychological impact of the new constructions in concrete, steel and glass was far greater here than in settled regions. The broad, asphalted streets and solid, multi-storied buildings, emblazoned with huge symbols and slogans, proclaimed the dawning of an age that self-confidently, brashly, rejected the fragile, uncertain existence of the past. The other aspect was the naming of cities, streets, parks and municipal buildings in honour of key figures and events in the socialist canon. For example, the townscape of Alma-Ata celebrated Karl Marx, Lenin, Kirov, Dzerzhinsky, Communism and the 50th Anniversary of the October Revolution; also 'progressive' Russian writers such as Belinsky and Gorky, and classical poets such as Pushkin and Lermontov. Comparatively few Kazakhs were so

---

53 A. Kanapin, *Kul'turnoye stroitel'stvo*, p. 291.
54 A. Kanapin, *Kul'turnoye stroitel'stvo*, p. 251.

honoured; of the few who were, most were writers, composers and other artists who had found favour with the regime (e.g. Abai, Kurmangazy, Auezov, Zhambul and Kulyash Baiseitova).[55] Tsarist settlements were given names that were more in keeping with the new age, reflecting either a Soviet (or proto-Soviet) connection or a local, national identification. Verny (literally, 'Faithful'), once a Tsarist fort, became (in 1921) Alma-Ata, a name derived from the ancient Kazakh term for the site; Fort Aleksandrovsky became Shevchenko; Akmolinsk, Tselinograd (Virgin Lands City). Thus, the very environment was explicitly and implicitly Sovietized.

Implementation 2: Destroying the old

The positive efforts to build a new society were accompanied by a devastating attack on all that was perceived to be representative of the past. There were three main thrusts in this campaign of destruction. Chronologically, the first was the liquidation of members of the liberal intellectual and political elite. After the formation of the KASSR, they joined forces with the new Soviet government, but were soon being accused of 'nationalistic tendencies'. A similar charge was levelled against a number of first-generation Kazakh Communists, who, driven by idealism rather than political ambition, dared to express their disapproval of some of the ill-conceived and ill-prepared measures that were introduced in the early 1920s (particularly the land and water reforms and the agricultural policies).

The first campaign of terror was unleashed in 1928 with the 'discovery' of an underground counter-revolutionary organization; mass arrests followed. The so-called 'leaders' of the movement were sentenced to five to eight years of exile and imprisonment. Those who survived this ordeal were re-arrested, along with many new suspects, in 1937. Most of the victims of this second wave of repression were shot in about 1938. They included many prominent members of the Kazakh intelligentsia.[56] Neither the number nor the fate of the many less prestigious individuals who were arrested during this period is known. There was a third wave of terror in 1949–50; most of the victims of this period, however, appear to have been imprisoned rather than executed and many were eventually released in the years following Stalin's death in 1953.

What the purges achieved is perhaps best summed up in the words of a child of one of the victims: 'to frighten and to shock the population, to break them and to check the

---

55 I. Malyar, *Ikh imenami ulitsy nazvali* (Alma-Ata, Zhalyn, 1983), gives a survey of the most commonly used names.
56 L. D. Kuderina, *Genotsid v Kazakhstane* (Moscow, Scorpion, 1994), pp. 47–53.

possibility of popular opposition'.[57] The purges also had an insidious effect on social cohesion, undermining personal loyalties by giving rein to fear, greed and malice; many years later, when records of the criminal proceedings became accessible, it was revealed that friends, neighbours and close relatives had often numbered amongst the denunciators. Together these three factors – the cowing of the population through fear, the elimination of alternative, possibly dissident sources of authority, and the sowing of the seeds of distrust and dissension – hugely accelerated the disintegrative processes that had already begun to take effect during the Tsarist period. Under Soviet rule, traditional structures were weakened to such an extent that if they retained any power at all (and whether they did or not is still a matter of debate), it was largely in the informal, private sphere. In public life, there was a mass transfer of allegiance to Soviet institutions; within two to three decades, this resulted in a number of Kazakhs making impressive careers not merely in the republican state/Party organizations, but in the central organs in Moscow.

The second prong of the attack was the eradication of pastoral nomadism through collectivization and sedentarization. This was in many respects the culmination of the policy of circumscription and integration of the nomad community that had been initiated by the Tsarist authorities. Under Soviet rule, the first stage in this process was the drawing of the Kazakhs into the planned, socialized economy as producers and as consumers. Compulsory procurement quotas rose dramatically; fairs continued to play an important role, helping to break the closed circle of the nomad economy by creating an ever-increasing demand for – and dependency on – processed and manufactured goods such as tea, sugar, matches, kerosene, clothes and shoes.[58] This trade was carried out in cash, which in turn hastened the monetarization of society. Opportunities for industrial work (e.g. on the Turksib railway line or in the Gur'yev oilfields) also increased. The nomads and semi-nomads were unable to keep pace with these new developments and their mass pauperization, which had begun in the nineteenth century, deepened. Matters were exacerbated by disastrous weather conditions, especially the zhut of 1927/8 in the Syr Darya region, which wiped out some 1.7 million head of livestock, almost one-third of the local flocks.[59]

Factors such as these were already changing the traditional way of life and beginning to encourage the Kazakhs to join the newly-established cooperatives. Nevertheless, in 1928 the state launched the second stage of the campaign, that of wholesale collectivization. It was part of an all-Union socio-economic crusade, but in Kazakhstan,

---

57 Kuderina, *Genotsid*, p. 58.
58 Zh. B. Abylkhozhin, *Traditsionnaya struktura Kazakhstana* (Alma-Ata, Gylym, 1991), p. 44–7. This work, which draws on archival material and rare publications of the 1920s, was one of the first to give a full and detailed account of the sedentarization period.
59 Zh.B. Abylkhozhin, *Traditsionnaya struktura*, p. 117.

because of the region's cultural and environmental peculiarities, it had a more devastating effect than in any of the other republics. It was initiated by a series of decrees that aimed to redistribute wealth, which generally met with limited success since they were ill-adapted to local conditions and violated the nomads' sense of community and natural justice: even the poorest were reluctant to take livestock that by rights belonged to others and many subsequently returned animals acquired in this manner to their original owners.[60]

The Party-state authorities responded by imposing increasingly punitive measures on wealthy 'bai-kulak' households. Since the effectiveness (and loyalty) of local officials was judged by the speed with which they could push through the collectivization and concomitant sedentarization programmes, there was a mad race to herd the population into the giant new collective farms. In 1928, only 2 per cent of all Kazakh households were collectivized; by April 1930, 50.5 per cent. By the spring of 1932, collectivization had been completed in the grain-producing northeast and the cotton-producing south of the republic; in the remaining regions it was completed by 1933.[61]

Throughout this period the state orders were constantly being increased. Complaints and protests from the local communities were ignored. 'Hoarding' (i.e. non-fulfilment of the quotas) was punishable by fines, prison sentences, or, in thousands of cases, death. The pressure was so relentless that in order to satisfy the wholly unrealistic state targets the nomads were forced to resort to such extreme measures as shearing their sheep in winter, which inevitably led to the decimation of their flocks.[62] By 1930 the situation had become so desperate that there were armed uprisings in many parts of the country. Some of the insurrectionists later joined forces with the Turkmen *basmachi* (guerrillas) in the south, while others fled abroad.

The cost of the collectivization campaign in terms of human and animal losses was calamitous: out of a Kazakh population of approximately 4,120,000 in 1930, some 1,750,000 had died from starvation, epidemics and executions by 1939 – over 40 per cent of the entire population (this is in addition to deaths from natural causes); 200,000 fled into neighbouring countries and remained there (another 400,000 fled, but later returned) and 453,000 took refuge in neighbouring Soviet republics, also to remain there permanently.[63] Even in 1959, the Kazakh population in Kazakhstan still numbered some one million less than it had in 1926 (2.8 million and 3.7 million respectively). The livestock losses were equally shocking: out of 6.5 million head of cattle in

---

60 Zh.B. Abylkhozhin, *Traditsionnaya struktura*, pp. 144–7.
61 *Istoriya*, II, p. 258. Zh.B. Abylkhozhin, p. 177.
62 Zh.B. Abylkhozhin, p. 184.
63 M.B. Tatimov, *Sotsial'naya obuslovlennost' demograficheskikh protsessov* (Alma-Ata, Nauka, 1989), pp. 120–6.

1928, less than one million were left in 1932; the numbers of sheep fell from 18.5 million to 1.5 million during this same period; of horses from 3.5 million to well under half a million; and of camels from one million to 63,000 (in 1935).[64] In 1932 a directive was issued to 'put right' the excesses of over-zealous officials, but by this time the damage was irreparable.

The tragedy of collectivization and sedentarization was not limited to the squandering of human and animal resources: it extended to the annihilation of a whole culture. The knowledge, skills and experience that had been accumulated over centuries were suddenly rendered less than worthless, taken now as measures of ignorance and 'primitiveness' rather than of high accomplishment. And in this collectivized, mechanized new world the most surefooted, eagle-eyed nomad was truly helpless. Factory-processed food was suddenly substituted for the traditional diet of fresh meat and dairy products. Even the family home was no longer the refuge that it had once been: prefabricated hutches, ranged in serried ranks along metalled roads, now replaced the tactile softness of the yurt, and equally, signalled the end of the personal freedom and the harmonious integration with the natural world that it had represented. The relatively few nomads who survived this brutal campaign were left disoriented and disempowered, no longer a force to be reckoned with.

The third major attack on traditional society was the campaign to eradicate Islam. This was part of an all-Union movement against religion. The civic nature of Islam, however, presented the authorities with problems that were very different from those encountered in the Christian communities of the European regions. In Kazakhstan, as elsewhere in Central Asia, society was permeated with Islamic institutions. In the early 1920s, many of the schools and colleges and most of the law courts in the newly founded KASSR were Muslim. The script used for Kazakh at this time was Arabic, the script of the holy Qur'an; the customs and rituals of everyday life were Muslim (or understood as such); the intellectual and political leaders of the community, including many Party members, identified themselves as Muslims; and Muslim religious leaders were, as acknowledged in Soviet sources of the time, active and influential at all levels of society.[65] It was not, therefore, a matter merely of attacking particular beliefs, but rather of rooting out the complex socio-cultural system which underpinned the tenets of faith.

In November (December) 1917, Lenin and Stalin jointly issued an appeal 'To All the Toiling Muslims of Russia and the East' which promised 'the Kirgiz (i.e. Kazakhs) and Sarts of Siberia and Turkestan', among others, that from that day forth their 'beliefs and customs, national and cultural institutions would be free and inviolate'. Barely

---

64 Zh.B. Abylkhozhin, *Traditsionnaya struktura*, p. 190.
65 A.K. Sultangaliyeva, 'Islam v Kazakhstane', *Vostok*, Moscow, no. 3, 1994, pp. 72–80.

three years later, however, the Tenth Party Congress (1921) passed a resolution calling for a comprehensive anti-religious campaign to be launched throughout the country. In Kazakhstan, Bolshevik power had not as yet been firmly established; hence it was necessary to proceed with some care at this stage in order to avoid offending local sensibilities and thus alienating the population. The early 1920s were characterized by a 'hearts and minds' struggle during which the authorities tried to discredit Islamic beliefs and practices, but in general not to ban them. There were cases where the zeal of individual officials led to bouts of excessively repressive action, but for the most part it was a period of mutual, albeit uneasy, accommodation. Muslim educational and legal institutions continued to function and it was still possible to apply for, and receive, permission to take time off to celebrate Muslim feasts.[66]

Meanwhile, the secular authorities were gathering information on the religious community and testing the success of their atheistic propaganda. By the second half of the decade official attitudes towards Islam began to harden. Muslim schools and law courts were phased out in favour of Soviet institutions; large numbers of mosques were closed and Islamic literature confiscated. Discriminatory legislation against clerics and preachers (of all faiths) was passed in 1928–9, as a result of which it became increasingly difficult for such individuals to find housing or employment. The Law of Religious Associations (which remained in force from 1929 to 1990) severely limited the rights of believers, making such activities as religious education, proselytizing and fund-raising illegal.[67] Meanwhile, anti-religious measures were intensified; these included the publication of vast quantities of anti-religious literature, the compulsory introduction of atheistic instruction into the educational curriculum, and the organization of alternative secular feasts to compete with religious events (e.g. a secular version of the end-of-Ramadan celebration). From around 1930, the anti-religious campaign merged with that of collectivization, and mass arrests and executions were used to eliminate Muslims as well as bais, 'hoarders' and other class enemies.

There is no documentary information available for this period and it is impossible to be sure precisely what happened at a grass-roots level. All that is known for certain is that during the Second World War the active persecution of believers was suspended and some concessions were made towards the main faiths, including Islam. The Muslim Spiritual Directorate of Central Asia and Kazakhstan was officially constituted in 1943; subsequently, a few mosques were reopened, and, under the strict supervision

---

66 The collection of archival documents published under the title of *Preodoloevoye religioznoye vliyaniye islama* (Alma-Ata, 1990), gives many such examples.
67 To put developments in Kazakhstan at this period in context, see P. Walters, 'A survey of Soviet religious policy', in S. Ramet (ed.), *Religious Policy in the Soviet Union* (Cambridge, CUP, 1993), pp. 3–30.

of the Spiritual Directorate, a small quantity of religious literature was printed. A few carefully selected Central Asians were eventually allowed to take part in the annual pilgrimage to Mecca. So far as the general mass of Kazakhs was concerned, most continued to identify themselves as Muslims, but their knowledge of Islam was almost non-existent. Some symbolic rituals were preserved (e.g. circumcision and funeral ceremonies), but very little else. Non-Muslim observers of Soviet Islam frequently surmised – or even asserted with confidence – that the faith was kept alive through these years by underground Sufi movements. Muslim visitors to the region, however, including a steady stream of students from Asian and African countries, who were able to travel far more widely than foreign Europeans, were invariably struck by the absence of any knowledge of Islamic beliefs or rituals, even of the basic declaration of faith ('There is no God but God and Muhammad is His Prophet').[68] This reveals a major difference in the perceptions of Muslims and non-Muslims as to what constitutes Islam. The latter took virtually any remnant of popular custom as evidence of the survival of Islam. Many Kazakhs during the Soviet period (and since) would describe themselves as 'atheists but also Muslims'. Such statements were made with no sense of irony. On the contrary, they were statements of what seemed to them to be a self-evident truth: namely, that Islam was part of their cultural heritage, a crucial bond between Kazakhs past, present and future, but not necessarily a bond between the individual and God, nor between Kazakhs and the supranational Muslim community of believers.

Consolidation of Soviet and national identities

It is a paradox, almost impenetrable for outsiders, that despite the dreadful sufferings of the 1930s, the majority of Kazakhs who survived the terror continued, like other Soviet citizens, to trust the regime. Yet any visitor to the region who has spoken to members of the older generation will realize that this was indeed a genuinely held conviction, not a pose adopted for officialdom. One of the factors which helped to strengthen this sense of allegiance was the experience of the Second World War (or in Soviet terminology, 'The Great Patriotic War'). Kazakh soldiers fought alongside representatives of many other Soviet nationalities, united with them in the common cause of defending the 'Motherland', a concept which embraced the national territory, but

---

68 From the late 1950s onwards students from countries such as Egypt, Algeria, India, Pakistan and later, Bangladesh, would regularly spend 5–6 years studying at institutes of higher education in Central Asia. The present author had discussions with many of them concerning their impressions of the region, including their assessment of the level of Islamic consciousness; she herself also made a number of visits to Central Asia and was able to make a personal evaluation of the situation.

extended beyond that to include the broader Soviet identity. Several divisions were raised in Kazakhstan, playing a heroic part in many actions, notably in the defence of Moscow in 1941, and becoming symbols of the Kazakh republic's wholehearted loyalty to the Union. The huge war memorial in the centre of Almaty remains an emotional focus for the republic's sense of civic pride, the place where brides lay their wreaths, soldiers swear their oaths of allegiance and schoolchildren come to parade and learn about their history.[69] The civilian population also made a major contribution to the war effort, raising industrial and agricultural production and giving homes to thousands of child evacuees from Moscow, Leningrad and other European centres. Many industrial and scientific enterprises were relocated from the exposed western front and their workers were likewise accepted into the local communities. Thus, in Kazakhstan, perhaps even more than in the other Soviet republics, the war was a time of all-Union integration, and also of consolidating a sense of national self-esteem.

A second important episode was that of the reclamation of the Virgin Lands in the 1950s. The aim of this grandiose scheme, the brainchild of Nikita Khrushchev, was to bring millions of hectares of untilled land under the plough in order to increase grain production. The Kazakh republican leaders at the time were opposed to the scheme, insisting that it was too big and too precipitate and that it would destroy the grasslands of the steppe. They were overruled, however, and the plan was put into action in 1954 under the direction of Panteleimon Ponomarenko and Leonid Brezhnev (who soon replaced the former as First Party Secretary of Kazakhstan). By 1955, the area under cultivation had been increased by two-and-a-half times, to a total of 20.6 million hectares. The project was portrayed as a military campaign and described in the same patriotic terms as the war effort. When in 1956 production reached the magic benchmark of 1 billion *pud* (over 16 million tonnes), medals were awarded to more than 387,000 workers;[70] in 1957, the republic was awarded the Order of Lenin in recognition of its achievement. Future harvests were often to fall far short of this level, owing to the unpredictable weather conditions and, later, severe soil degradation and erosion. However, the vision of colossal, awe-inspiring advances had already been firmly implanted in people's minds, fusing with the heroic images of wartime exploits to create a sense of almost superhuman power.

The Virgin Lands were located in the central-northern steppes, a depopulated area once home to the nomads but now inhabited mainly by deported Volga Germans,

---

69 G. Musrepov's popular novel, *Soldier From Kazakhstan*, first published in 1948 in Kazakh, then in 1949 in Russian, was the literary equivalent of the monument, portraying the sense of patriotism and loyalty to the Soviet Union through the story of a young Kazakh from Gur'yev.
70 J. Dornberg, *Brezhnev: The Masks of Power* (London, André Deutsch, 1974), pp. 135–41, gives a vivid picture of the huge, chaotic enterprise.

Chechens and other 'punished peoples'. The rehabilitation of these deportees coincided with the launch of the Virgin Lands campaign and many of them stayed on in their places of exile to take part in this new venture.[71] Over the next few years about half a million volunteers flooded into the republic, attracted by the high wages and special benefits that were being offered. The latter soon proved to be illusory and the newcomers found themselves living in desperate conditions, though the situation gradually improved and the influx of doctors, engineers and other professionals helped to raise standards throughout the region. The Kazakh population, at least in public utterances, made little protest at the destruction of the grasslands. Doubtless this was largely because such action would have been ignored and would, moreover, have invited the very real danger of state reprisals. There were, however, other factors. One was the excitement and challenge that was generated by this struggle with nature. Another seems to have been a desire on the part of at least some Kazakhs to distance themselves from their 'backward' nomadic past; for them, the empty expanses that had once been the living fabric of Kazakh existence were no more than a dead memory, drained of emotional significance. Instead, the steppe was now regarded as a potential source of unlimited wealth, to be tamed rather than, as in the nomad period, to be respected and husbanded.

---

71 A comparison of the census reports for 1926 and 1959 indicates that approximately half a million Volga Germans must have been deported to Kazakhstan during the war.

5 REDISCOVERY AND REDEFINITION: TOWARDS A NEW NATIONAL IDENTITY

By the 1970s the Kazakhs were arguably the most thoroughly Sovietized of all Soviet citizens – and the overwhelming majority appeared to be proud of this. The titular people of the second largest republic (after the RSFSR) in the USSR, they could look back on fifty years of economic and social achievement. Much of this had been accomplished at the cost of very considerable suffering, but by this period there was sufficient stability and prosperity for most people to feel that the effort had been worthwhile: those who might have had doubts knew better than to voice them in private, let alone in public. The popular image of the republic, as described in countless textbooks, brochures and documentary films was of 'A Storehouse of Natural Riches ... of Great Transformations ... A Republic of Major Industries ... of Collective Farms and State Farms ... A Land with a Great Future.'[72] The Kazakhs had universal literacy and the highest percentage of graduates with tertiary education of all the Central Asian peoples. Dinmukhamed Kunayev (1912–93), who became Kazakh First Party Secretary in 1960, did much to enhance their position. A protégé and close personal associate of Leonid Brezhnev, he became a candidate member of the Politburo of the Central Committee of the Communist Party of the Soviet Union in 1966, and a full member in 1971 – an achievement, unique amongst Central Asian Party leaders, which gave him enormous power and influence; this in turn benefited Kazakhstan, since he was able to manipulate the system in such a way as to protect and further its interests. It was under his leadership (which, with a small hiatus in the early 1960s, lasted for over twenty years), that Kazakhstan consolidated its position as a key republic, one of the Soviet state's crucial fuel and power centres, a large-scale producer of grain and meat, and the location of a sizeable portion of the nuclear arsenal and space research programme. Although it was one of the most ethnically mixed of all the republics, with the Kazakhs themselves representing less than 40 per cent of the total population, race relations were generally harmonious and Kazakhstan prided itself on its

---

[72] N. Yanios, B. Dvoskin, *Besedy o Kazakhstane* (Alma-Ata, Kazgosizdat, 1957) is a typical example of the type of didactic-propaganda material that was produced at this time.

reputation as an outstanding example of 'internationalism'. This was evidenced by, among other things, a relatively high proportion of inter-ethnic marriages (by 1970 almost 25 per cent in urban areas).

Cultural survivals

By this time, very little of the pre-Soviet culture remained alive in everyday life. Male and female dress was wholly European, only occasionally embellished with some form of more or less traditional headgear in the more distant rural districts. Islamic practices had been almost entirely eradicated; if observed at all, they were regarded as a form of superstition, or something that was required by convention, but that no longer possessed any spiritual significance for the participants. So far as the performing arts were concerned, a few bards maintained the art of reciting the heroic epics, but for the general public, 'traditional' art was represented by the music and dance groups that performed frothy selections of Kazakhified European, or Europeanized Kazakh items, dressed in mass-produced, token approximations of 'native costume'. Even the knowledge of the language had by now been eroded to the point where the majority of young, urban-based Kazakhs knew no more than standard colloquial phrases in Kazakh. Nevertheless, there was still a strong awareness of a specifically Kazakh identity, even if this was based more in self-perception rather than in identifiable cultural indicators. Thus, in the 1970 census, for example, 98 per cent of Kazakhs claimed Kazakh as their mother tongue, while only just over 40 per cent admitted to 'a fluent knowledge of Russian as a second language', responses which surely reflected ethnic loyalty more than the actual linguistic situation.

One of the few areas in which a degree of continuity was preserved was food. The general diet was much the same as in any other part of the Soviet Union – namely, whatever was available at any given time – but there were a few local specialities such as horse meat and fat-tailed sheep. In particular, there was *bes parmak* ('five fingers'), a mixture of boiled meat and strips of dough that acquired the status of national dish, partly because it was felt to be uniquely Kazakh (whereas a rice dish such as *plov* was shared by the neighbouring peoples), partly because it was a communal dish, made in large quantities, and thus symbolized the qualities of hospitality, expansiveness and community spirit that were an intrinsic part of the Kazakh self-image.

Another area in which tradition survived as a marker of ethnicity was burial practices. The rituals of washing and laying in the grave were mostly Islamic, but the vaulted, turreted, conical-domed or cube-like mausoleums that were erected over the tombs were a link to a much older past. These remote necropolises, sited on bare, windswept hilltops, looking from afar like miniature cities, bore strange witness to an inner world, utterly private, untouched by Soviet mores.

A third area in which there was a perceptible continuity was that of social interaction. Respect for senior members of society was deeply ingrained and entailed not only a display of formal courtesy, but also a deferential ceding of personal wishes and opinions. Within the family group, relationships were likewise regulated by convention, with a delicate balance between gender-specific spheres of action and authority. Marriage, as in the past, was strictly exogamous, with no consanguinity in the paternal line permitted within seven generations. This necessitated an active knowledge of family genealogy, which in turn helped to locate the individual in a wider social and historical context. Obligations of loyalty, support and protection to the kin-group (on the maternal as well as the paternal sides) continued to play an important role: familism became a defence mechanism, shielding the individual (as far as was possible) from the brutalities of the totalitarian system.

Outside the nuclear family there was a proliferation of analogous types of social networks, involving varying degrees of mutual loyalty and obligation. Some of these groupings were based on extended family links, and thus to a certain degree utilized the clan-tribal structures of the past. However, these new networks, which later, confusingly, came to be known in popular parlance as 'clans' (using the Russian/English term, not any of the traditional Kazakh terms), were far more diverse than those of the pre-Soviet era. They drew on a wide range of social relationships, such as, for example, school-friends, military service comrades, neighbours, people from the same town, work, Komsomol and Party contacts. Generally, but not exclusively, they were held together by a perception of mutual interests and mutual benefits.

Ethnic revival

It was in the 1970s that more concrete symbols of Kazakh cultural identity began to reappear. The most important of these was the yurt. In the past it had been the focal point of the communal life of the family: it had required constant maintenance and repair, hence care of the fabric had constituted an essential part of the regular work routine; it had been the setting for most social activities and was governed by strict rules of etiquette, expressing in spatial terms the ordering of society; it was, moreover, imbued with a mystical significance, the dome being interpreted as the material counterpart of the vault of the heavens, and the wooden supports – the trellis, the roof struts and the wheel of the smoke-hole – as the elements which determined whether there was to be harmony or chaos.[73] The smoke-hole wheel, the linch-pin of the edifice, was regarded as something so sacred that when oaths were sworn, the parties con-

---

73 Zh.K. Karakuzova, M.Sh. Khasanov, *Kosmos*, p. 18.

cerned would look up at it. Sons took care of the smoke-hole wheel from their father's yurt and handed it on from one generation to the next as a revered heirloom.[74]

With collectivization and sedentarization the yurt had become obsolete and the complex of beliefs, activities and codes of conduct that had been linked to it had been destroyed. It was only in the remoter areas of central and southern Kazakhstan that the shepherds who took the flocks to distant summer pastures continued to use simplified versions of the traditional yurt. In the 1950s, it began to resurface in villages and urban-type settlements as a portable outhouse, erected alongside the main home, to serve as an overspill area for storage, guest accommodation and other purposes requiring additional space. At this stage the yurt fulfilled a predominantly utilitarian function and little attention was paid to its cultural and aesthetic potential. In the 1960s, however, it acquired the status of an ethnic badge. The demand grew so rapidly that a number of factories were set up to manufacture yurts.[75] They were by no means cheap: even one that was made of synthetic materials and unlikely to last more than a few years would cost nearly 1,000 roubles, a very considerable outlay at a time when the average monthly wage was under 170 roubles.[76] By the 1970s, the use of yurts had expanded from the private domain into the public, where they were widely used as clubs, libraries, restaurants and exhibition centres. Soon, at least one sparkling white, sumptuously (albeit unconventionally) decorated yurt would grace every official ceremony and public celebration.

There was a similar rediscovery of traditional designs and handicrafts. These were originally revived in order to produce souvenirs for tourists and for export abroad. However, they soon became extremely popular within Kazakhstan itself and several factories were employed in the manufacture of felt rugs, woven girdles, wooden toys, ceramic dishes and beakers, stamped leather ornaments, miniature yurts and musical instruments. One of the most popular items was a *kumys* (fermented mare's milk) service,[77] which attempted to combine continuity of utensil design with continuity of consumption. The shape and decoration of these and other such 'traditional' objects had as much historical authenticity as the tartan wrapper on a packet of Scottish shortbread but, like the tartan (and the shortbread), even in their crudest, most commercialized and perfunctory form they still served as emblems of identity. During the 1980s this heightened interest in ethnic roots, and the desire to rediscover the cultural world of the past, also led to the appearance of increasing numbers of publications on subjects such as the meaning and origin of Kazakh personal names, the art of hunting

---

74 V.V. Vostrov, I.V. Zakharova, *Kazakhskoye narodnoye zhilishche* (Alma-Ata, Nauka, 1989), p. 36.
75 Ibid., p. 170.
76 *Narodnoye khozyaystvo Kazakhstana za 70 let*, p. 32.
77 M.S. Mukanov, *Kazakhskaya yurta* (Alma-Ata, Kainar, 1981), pp. 192–200.

with birds of prey, and the design of traditional dwellings. High-quality recordings of heroic epics were more readily available, and the opening of a well-stocked Museum of Traditional Kazakh Musical Instruments went some way towards cultivating an understanding of genuine folk music.

December 1986

It was against this background of an emerging awareness of ethnic identity that the demonstration of December 1986 erupted. It sent shock-waves throughout the Soviet Union, coming as it did long before the much more violent occurrences in other republics in 1988–91. The circumstances surrounding this incident remain obscure. The sequence of events, in so far as they can be ascertained, are as follows. In December 1986, the Kazakh Dinmukhamed Kunayev was summarily removed from his post as First Party Secretary of the Communist Party of Kazakhstan, and replaced by Gennady Kolbin, a Russian with no previous knowledge of the republic. In the past such a manoeuvre would not have attracted public attention (Leonid Brezhnev, after all, had been drafted in under similar circumstances some thirty years previously), but in the freer climate of the Gorbachev era it was unexpected, and aroused a general sense of concern and dissatisfaction. On 17 December, shortly after the appointment had been officially confirmed, groups of youths, mostly students, began to converge on the central square of the capital to request or demand an explanation from the Party leadership. The authorities were at first unsure how to respond. Kunayev was told that Gorbachev 'categorically forbade Kunayev to have a meeting with the young people'. Since Kolbin also refused to go out to them, it was left to three other senior officials, Mukashev, Nazarbayev and Kamalidenov, to respond. According to an eyewitness account,[78] they went out to the rostrum together and Nazarbayev, as spokesman for the group, explained that they had all supported Kolbin's appointment as First Secretary. The young people interrupted with shouts of 'We don't want to talk to you traitors' and began pelting him and his two companions with snowballs. Shortly after, a small delegation of five or six of the demonstrators was taken to meet Kolbin. Who these people were and what happened to them thereafter remains a mystery. The crowd became more restive and some fighting broke out (or was provoked by members of the KGB). The leadership either panicked or, more probably, was waiting for such an opportunity: the tanks were sent in and several people were fatally injured. A number of the demonstrators were arrested and some later sentenced to long terms of imprisonment, one of them committing suicide while in detention.

---

78 Karshil Asanov, *Pravda o perestroike v Kazakhstane*, I (Alma-Ata, privately printed, 1991), pp. 185–6.

Investigations, recriminations, calls for apologies, retrials and rehabilitations continued for years, but full details of the criminal proceedings were never made public. Theories were rife as to who was behind the incident, and why. The explanation that many Kazakhs at the time rejected, including those who had been present during the incident, was that it was an anti-Russian demonstration. Even such a fiercely independent champion of Kazakh culture as Karishal Asanov considered such a suggestion to be a slur on the good name of the Kazakh people.[79] Nevertheless, in the months that followed many Kazakhs did come to feel that those December days had marked a watershed in Russian–Kazakh relations; for all their protestations of amity and fraternal assistance, the Russian community remained silent when the Kazakh demonstrators were being subjected to excessively rough treatment, as though their liberal, pro-democracy views did not extend to the Kazakhs. This sense of exclusion, rejection and betrayal was the starting point for a fundamental reappraisal of the 'great friendship': the consequences of this shift were not immediately apparent but eventually it led to a distinct divergence between the political interests of the two groups. In the case of the Kazakhs, this merged with the growing awareness of ethnic identity, providing the impetus for the emergence of a nationalistic trend in public opinion.

Socio-political movements

The December 1986 demonstration resulted in a general reimposition of rigid political conformity. Even highly respected poets such as Olzhas Suleimenov and Mukhtar Shakhanov, who had previously been allowed a certain latitude, were now pressurized into a public affirmation of their support for the government. By 1989, however, the democratization process, already well under way in the western republics of the Soviet Union, started to penetrate Kazakhstan. This coincided with the appointment of Nursultan Nazarbayev to the post of First Party Secretary. Small socio-political groupings began to take shape. The first to be formally registered was the Nevada-Semipalatinsk anti-nuclear movement. The driving force behind it was Olzhas Suleimenov, an energetic, charismatic figure with a long-established record of commitment to civil rights issues. A product of Soviet 'internationalism', he was a Kazakh who spoke and wrote in Russian and was in many ways more at home in a Russian environment than a Kazakh one, yet at the same time had sufficient love and knowledge of the history of his people to feel deeply indignant at the manner in which they

---

79 The Praesidium of the Supreme Soviet passed a resolution on 24 September 1990, specifically stating that nationalism had played no part in the incident; also, that the participants were not, initially, breaking the law in any way. Blame for the disturbance was placed firmly at the door of the central government and the leadership of the republic.

were so often portrayed as culturally inferior, less developed than the Russians. His literary-historical work *Az i Ya* (a pun on the Russian pronoun *ya*, 'I', and 'Asia'), which sought to awaken an awareness of the Turkic contribution to Slav culture, appeared in Alma-Ata in 1975, and almost immediately attracted a storm of hostile criticism from Moscow. This gained him a reputation as a Kazakh nationalist, but his intention was not to reject the Russian legacy, but rather to reinstate a proper understanding of Kazakh culture. The Nevada-Semipalatinsk movement reflected this inclusive approach, involving people from all walks of life and all ethnic groups.

The other movements which began to appear at this time (around 1990) were, for the most part, mono-ethnic and overtly nationalistic. The main Kazakh groups were *Azat* ('Freedom'), *Alash* (the name of the legendary father of the Kazakh nation, also of the pre-Soviet 'bourgeois nationalist' movement), and *Zheltoksan* ('December'), originally formed as a pressure group to obtain a fair hearing for those who had been imprisoned after the December 1986 demonstration, but later becoming a more general opposition group. The leadership of these movements changed frequently and they had little popular support, but they did give voice to a growing undertow of anti-Russian sentiment. The sharpest public expression of this was the several-hundred-strong rally held in Alma-Ata in September 1990, shortly after the seventieth anniversary of the founding of the KASSR, at which banners expressing militantly nationalist slogans were on display.[80] Official attitudes towards these movements fluctuated between repression and limited toleration. They gradually succeeded in producing and distributing their own broadsheets, albeit intermittently and in the face of great practical difficulties. However, they were still far from constituting an effective opposition, and in the 1991 presidential election Nursultan Nazarbayev stood unopposed and was elected President by an almost one hundred per cent vote.

Islam

There was a cautious revival of interest in Islam, analogous to that which was emerging in other parts of Central Asia, but largely independent and spontaneous. It received some support from senior Kazakh officials and in 1990 resulted in the establishment of a separate muftiat in Alma-Ata, still within the framework of the Soviet Islamic hierarchy, but no longer under the jurisdiction of the Tashkent-based Muslim Spiritual Directorate of Central Asia. This was the first step towards an official acknowledgment of the Islamic element in the national heritage. Simultaneously, individual Kazakhs began to rediscover Islam not simply as part of their general historical

---

80 Report in *Summary of World Broadcasts*, SU/0882 B/9, 29 September 1990 [9].

and cultural background, but as a living source of moral and spiritual inspiration. Mostly students and educated young professionals, they began seeking out scholarly information about the religion and tried to live their lives according to the teachings of Islam; for the women, this included adopting, in so far as was practical, a modified Islamic dress code. Relatively few in number (in the capital, there were probably no more than 20–30 sympathizers), they nevertheless formed an outspoken opposition to the official Islamic hierarchy, whose representatives they regarded as hypocrites and lackeys of the state.[81] They launched a periodical entitled *Khak* ('Truth'), in November 1991; registered and printed in Moscow, it appeared at irregular intervals. The masthead bore the legend 'Islamic Political Newspaper' and a quotation from the Qur'an. The print run of the first issue was recorded as 100,000 copies, but by the third issue this had been reduced to 20,000; thereafter it appears to have ceased publication. It supported the newly-founded (or, as its members insisted, re-established) *Alash* party, and was extremely hostile to the Kazakh establishment, including Nursultan Nazarbayev (branded as 'a traitor')[82] and the Kazakh Mufti Ratbek Nysanbayev. Such extremism did much to discredit the revivalists in the eyes of the great majority of Kazakhs, whose attitude towards Islam was, at this stage, primarily one of passive rather than active interest.

Language revival and historical revision

Two other areas in which there was a determined reassertion of Kazakh identity were language and historical interpretation. Urban Kazakhs who had formerly prided themselves on their excellent command of Russian now began to feel a sense of embarrassment and deprivation that their knowledge of their mother tongue was so limited and ungrammatical. There was a growing demand for Kazakh-medium kindergartens and schools, also for grammars, phrasebooks, dictionaries and other teaching materials. It became a point of honour to use the language as much as possible, even if only in the exchange of greetings and simple pleasantries. The *Qazaq tili* (Kazakh language) movement helped to channel this new linguistic sensitivity into an organized campaign to have Kazakh formally designated the state language of the republic (no language had held this status before). This was achieved in September 1989, at about the same time that the titular languages of other Soviet republics were being given this recognition. Thereafter, Kazakh was increasingly used in the public domain (though generally still in tandem with Russian, which remained the language of 'inter-ethnic communication').

---

81 See, for example, leading article in *Khak*, no. 3, 1992, p. 1.
82 In *Khak*, no. 2, 1991, in the leading article by Aron Atabek (p. 1), President Nazarbayev is described as 'a collaborator in Kolbin's crimes'.

The aspect of the reappraisal of Kazakh history that had the greatest popular appeal was that relating to clan-tribal issues. For over sixty years the official attitude towards the clan-tribal system was that it was primitive, repressive and a bar to progress, and must therefore be destroyed. Underlying this was the fear that these traditional structures could be used as subversive power bases which might threaten the security of the new regime. Consequently, in public Kazakhs were careful to distance themselves from any possible association with clan-tribal factions and vehemently to condemn signs of group solidarity formed on this basis. In private, however, knowledge of family genealogy, with its inevitable association with clan-tribal formations, retained its importance, not necessarily constituting an active socio-political force (though in Central Asia it certainly helped to maintain nepotism and other types of kinship patronage), but more as a passive expression of identity, an ethnic 'passport'. In the late 1980s such questions began to be discussed more openly and placed in the broader context of Kazakh social history.

Professional historians, meanwhile, were slowly embarking on a re-evaluation of Kazakh–Russian relations. It was acknowledged that much relevant archival material had been suppressed during the Soviet period; also, that there had been deliberate distortions, omissions and ideologically biased interpretations. Consequently, a simplified version of events had been propagated in which Kazakh protagonists were portrayed in a positive light if they supported Russian interests, but were 'cruel', 'despotic' and 'greedy' if they opposed them. The *perestroika* historians called for a more critical approach, with greater attention being paid to the motives of the Kazakhs.[83] One of the most significant developments was the change in attitude towards the 'bourgeois nationalists' of the Alash group, who were now treated with a new respect. An even more important shift was the open admission of the suffering that had been inflicted on the Kazakh population during the period of collectivization and sedentarization; this had previously been either ignored or passed over with vague statements about mistakes and misunderstandings. Kazakh demographers at last began to publish detailed estimates of the numbers of people who perished at that time.

---

83 Proceedings of the 'Round Table' Conference held in July 1990, summarized in *Natsional'nyye dvizheniya v usloviakh Kolonializma* (Tselinograd, al-Farabi, 1991), pp. 114–19.

6 INDEPENDENT KAZAKHSTAN

The articulation of a Kazakh national consciousness gained momentum throughout the 1980s, but it had not yet matured into a liberation movement when the Soviet Union suddenly disintegrated at the end of 1991. Consequently, there was no freedom struggle: the Kazakhs were bereft both of the organizational experience of such a period of preparation, and of the ideological bonding of the fight for a common national goal; hence, there was no legacy of audacious deeds to celebrate, no emotive slogans and symbols, no heroes, no national myths. A belated declaration of independence was made on 16 December 1991, a week after the announcement that the Slav republics were establishing a separate Commonwealth of their own. A summit meeting was hastily convened in Alma-Ata on 20–21 December, at which it was agreed that Kazakhstan, along with seven other former Soviet republics, would be admitted to an enlarged Commonwealth of Independent States (CIS).

The initial reaction of the great majority of the Kazakh population was one of disbelief, mixed with chronic anxiety. Within a few months, however, a more optimistic mood was beginning to emerge. This was in large measure due to the skill with which President Nazarbayev handled the transition from Soviet republic to independent statehood. He succeeded in projecting an image of stability, but also of flexibility and commitment to political and economic reform. His personal charm and obvious ability, along with the many human and material resources of the new state, rapidly won for Kazakhstan a pre-eminent position among the former Soviet republics. Politicians, businessmen and civil servants round the globe learnt how to locate Almaty on the map. Flights from exotic places such as Frankfurt and Bangkok began to arrive at the airport that until a few months previously had only had to cope with domestic traffic. Elegant foreign cars and the badges of foreign embassies became commonplace sights, while hotel lobbies and restaurants echoed to the sound of impatient foreign customers demanding instant attention. Kazakhs, too, began to travel abroad in increasing numbers, first in delegations, later as individuals on a variety of public and private missions. In short, Kazakhstan had suddenly gained acceptance as a full member of the international community.

This had a dramatic effect on the Kazakhs' self-esteem. For decades they had lived in the Russian shadow, suffering the confidence-sapping indignity of the label 'younger brother', the patent implication of which was that they were less advanced and less cultured than the Slav 'elder brother'. Yet now, as the titular people of this newly independent state, they were courted by world statesmen and senior managers of transnational corporations. Moreover, they were deemed to have negotiated the chaos caused by the collapse of the Soviet Union with such success that the Kazakh example was increasingly held up as a model for other former Soviet republics, including Russia, to emulate. Kazakhs, whether businessmen or tourists, sportsmen or scientists, no longer had to describe themselves to strangers as 'a type of Russian'; they had become a known nation in their own right.

The emblems and institutions of Soviet Kazakhstan had been formulated in such a way as to underline the subordinacy of the republic to the Union. After a brief period of readjustment these were replaced by a different set of symbols that clearly proclaimed the emergence of independent Kazakhstan; these included a national flag, anthem, constitution, central bank, (embryonic) defence forces, currency, passports and other such formal attributes of statehood. The cultural references were drawn from Kazakh traditions. The new flag, for example, includes a band of Kazakh ornamental motifs and a representation of the steppe eagle, favoured hunting companion of the Kazakhs of old; the main elements of the national coat-of-arms are the winged horses of Kazakh myth and the sacred smoke-hole wheel of the yurt. The national colours of blue and gold, representing the sky and the sun, have a universal significance, but also a symbolic link to the ancient Kazakh cult of the Sky God. Likewise, cities, streets and other public places began to be renamed so as to emphasize the Kazakh context. The Caspian port of Shevchenko, for example, has now become Aktau; Tselinograd, Gur'yev and Panfilov are now Akmola, Atyrau and Zharkent respectively. In the capital alone, by 1995 over twenty streets had been renamed: Kommunistichesky was transformed into Ablai Khan; Karl Marx into D. Kunayev; and Kirov into Bogenbai batyr. The spelling of the names of several towns and provinces was also altered to reflect Kazakh pronunciation; the official designation of Chimkent, for example, has become Shymkent; Alma-Ata is now Almaty and Kustanai, Kostanai.[84]

Aspects of post-Soviet Kazakh identity

For over a century, Kazakh history and culture has been defined through Russian perceptions. As discussed above, this took place in two stages. Under Tsarist rule,

---

84 By a decree of the Supreme Kenges (Parliament) of Kazakhstan, passed on 14 May 1993.

Russian influence was strong, but still partial and to some extent heterogeneous; under Soviet rule, it was uniform and all-embracing. During this second period the Kazakh national myth was forged to fit a paradigm of socio-political development in strict accordance with Marxist-Leninist doctrine. In the last decades of the Soviet era there were signs of an ethnic revival, but this was mainly concerned with the rediscovery and reassertion of an indigenous cultural identity. Only a handful of individuals were prepared openly to question the authenticity of the established historical edifice and very few indeed were beginning to contemplate the proposition that 'the political and the national unit should be congruent'; such nationalist tendencies as did exist were still very tentative, with no clear goals.

The collapse of the Soviet Union destroyed the entire context – cultural, economic, political and ideological – within which the modern Kazakh identity had been formed. Suddenly, all the assumptions that previously had been taken for granted, from the conventional value judgments on Kazakh culture to the legitimacy of the Kazakh republic (which was, after all, a Soviet creation), were called into question. It was as necessary as it was inevitable that there should be a refashioning of the national identity in order to give meaning to this newly acquired independence, to enable the Kazakhs, as individuals and as a group, to relate to the post-Soviet environment. The abrupt removal of Russian/Soviet pressure unleashed a soul-searching debate on what, to Kazakhs, constituted 'Kazakh-ness'. Numerous academic works as well as articles and letters in the popular press have been devoted to this subject over the past few years, charting the evolution of the new national narrative. The process is still at an early stage, but two interlinked priorities are emerging: one is to establish a pre-Soviet legitimacy for the Kazakh state and its existing territorial boundaries; the other is to bridge the profound rupture between past and present that was inflicted on the Kazakh people as a result of Soviet developmental policies.

The official post-Soviet nation-building project employs many of the devices of the Soviet period such as, for example, the rewriting of history (a new multi-volume work is currently in preparation), the renaming of public places, the introduction of new emblems, institutions and cultural manifestations, and the elevation of the national language. As to the substance of the new national myth, however, there is as yet very little that has been added or removed from the Soviet version; rather, it is the emphasis that has been altered. Thus, for example, the emergence of the Kazakh Khanate in the fifteenth century is now being promoted as the birth of Kazakh statehood; the 540th anniversary of this event (which cannot, in fact, be attributed to a precise date) was celebrated in 1995.[85] The importance that is currently being as-

---

85 *Kazakhstanskaya pravda*, 8 July 1995.

cribed to the founding of the Khanate underlines the difficulty that faces this new generation of nation-builders – namely, the relative paucity of unifying elements. Historical figures such as Ablai Khan make somewhat ambiguous heroes and, moreover, may even be regarded as divisive, since they could be seen to represent the interests of one Horde rather than of the Kazakh people as a whole.[86] For some of the other Central Asian peoples, the literary heritage, oral or written, provides a focus for the national identity; for the Kirghiz, for example, the Manas epic has traditionally constituted the defining feature of their group identity, cutting across regional and tribal differences. The Kazakhs have nothing that is comparable to this: almost all their oral epics are part of the common Central Asian fund, while their written literature, though distinctive and original, is stylistically too indebted to Russian/Soviet models to serve this purpose. The nineteenth-century 'enlighteners', who were instrumental in shaping the notion of the Kazakhs as a discrete national entity, are also no longer accorded universal approbation: Shokan Valikhanov in particular is felt by some to have been too enthusiastic an advocate of Russian culture.

Two events in modern Kazakh history which might have acted as defining experiences have, to date, made relatively little impact. One is the collectivization-sedentarization campaign which, in per capita terms, rates among the most horrific acts of carnage of the twentieth century. This is now acknowledged and Kazakhs will often refer to it themselves in such terms. Yet they do so with a curious sense of detachment, as though it were not located in actual, recorded, time, but rather in some abstract past. Perhaps because whole sectors of the population were wiped out and there were few family survivors to keep alive memories of the dead; perhaps because the remainder of the population was subjected to intense and unchallenged propaganda which depicted the episode in glowing, optimistic terms; perhaps because the modern way of life was created in the vacuum left by the destruction of the old; perhaps because the disaster was so great that it could not be consciously comprehended and was therefore blocked out – perhaps for these and any number of other, unfathomable, reasons, the tragedy of the 1930s has not, for the Kazakhs, assumed the centrality that the Genocide has acquired in the Armenian consciousness, or the Holocaust in the Jewish. The Virgin Lands campaign, which resulted in an analogous destruction of the natural environment, evoked some opposition at the time but, again, was soon justified, accepted and absorbed into the catalogue of positive achievements. It is possible that in the future, mobilizers of public opinion will sensitize these issues, imbuing them with national significance, but as yet they remain uninterpreted and in a way non-existent periods in the national experience.

---

86 Valikhanov, *Sobranie sochineneii*, IV, pp. 111–16.

Of the concepts which have emerged as defining factors over the past few years, four have assumed particular prominence. One of these is Islam, although for the great majority of Kazakhs today this continues to have a symbolic rather than a spiritual significance. There has been a slight increase in formal displays of piety. Many Kazakhs now make a point of refusing to eat (at least in public) dishes which contain pork or lard. The Islamic prohibition on the drinking of alcohol, however, is honoured more in the breach than the observance. Regular attendance at mosques remains low and there is little interest in institutions based on religious principles such as, for example, Islamic banking (although one of the first foreign banks to open a branch in Almaty was in fact the Saudi-Kazakh joint venture *al-Baraka*). Members of the Kazakh Muftiat, the official Muslim organization, play a constant, though not particularly prominent role in public ceremonies. A Kazakh-language periodical entitled *Iman* ('Faith') has been produced by the Muftiat since 1992; a few other official publications are also sporadically available, including a Kazakh translation of the Qur'an.

Within this general context of what might be termed benign apathy towards Islam, there are some signs of a more active revival of interest in the faith. This is partly owing to the efforts of countless missionaries from Egypt, Turkey, Saudi Arabia, Pakistan and other Muslim countries. There is also, however, a spontaneous indigenous movement to rediscover Islam led by groupings such as Alash, which combine political opposition with a strong Islamic bias. However, they have singularly failed to attract public support. An attempt to create a Kazakh League of Muslim Women soon collapsed amid accusations of financial irregularities and internal power struggles. Other efforts have been more sustained; since independence a considerable number of local communities have contributed substantial funds for the building of mosques and Muslim cultural centres. Over the past three to four years several thousand students have taken up scholarships to study abroad at Muslim universities, and a certain amount of Muslim education, at primary and advanced level, is now available within Kazakhstan. Such undertakings receive some support from the state, as well as from Muslims abroad (e.g. from Kuwait and Egypt),[87] but much is financed from private, local sources. A number of Kazakhs have undertaken the prescribed pilgrimage to Mecca, but the exorbitant cost of the journey has been a severe deterrent. There is no evidence of the active involvement of Sufi orders in this re-Islamicization process, but some semi-academic semi-religious groups devoted to the study of the philosophy of the mystics have begun to appear.[88]

It is difficult to form any accurate impression of the regional spread of this new wave of Islamic consciousness. The general perception is that over the past few years

---

87 See, for example, *Aziya*, no. 24, 25 June 1993; *Aziya*, no. 45, 29 November 1993.
88 *Kazakhstanskaya pravda*, 3 February, 1993.

there has been an increase in all forms of Islamic activity in the south, centred on Turkestan, the burial place of the renowned and much-revered mystic Ahmad Yasavi, and on cities such as Shymkent, which have large populations of Uzbeks, who are commonly considered to be more devout than the Kazakhs. However, it is worth noting that newspaper reports often refer to examples of Islamic activities in the urban centres of the north, in districts such as Akmola, Kostanai, Turgay and Karaganda, where there are large Russian populations. Whether this is a balanced reflection of current trends or part of a political agenda to raise the visibility of Kazakh culture in the north is impossible to say. It is interesting to recall that in the early twentieth century it was chiefly in these areas, where Kazakhs were in direct contact with Russians, that Islam began to emerge as a powerful 'boundary marker' of identity and to assume some political significance. It is not inconceivable that a similar process is taking place today.

A second element that is regarded as a defining feature of contemporary Kazakh identity is Turkic-ness. Pan-Turkism enjoyed a certain popularity in Kazakhstan in the early twentieth century, notably among members of the Alash movement.[89] It was fiercely repressed during the Soviet period, but began to re-emerge in the 1980s. The new opposition parties, especially Azat and (the re-established) Alash, adopted pan-Turkic sentiments as part of their political agenda, along with some degree of pan-Islamism (mainly espoused by Alash); these affiliations were signalled by the use of such symbols as the star and crescent, the wolf's head (a common Turkic symbol) and, in the case of Alash, use of the Arabic script or of an Arabicized form of the Cyrillic script in their logotype. Since independence, general awareness of a shared Turkic culture has been strengthened by the wide variety of links that have been developed with Turkey. Several thousand Kazakh students have been awarded scholarships to study in Turkey and a number of Turkish-Kazakh schools and colleges have been established in Kazakhstan. Numerous collaborative projects have been initiated, including the compilation of bilingual Kazakh-Turkish dictionaries.

There are extensive state and private-sector economic joint ventures; these have been given added impetus by President Nazarbayev's admonition to 'focus on Turkey as a potential market and as an example of the development of a market economy'.[90] Turkish politicians have tended to stress the concept of 'the brotherhood of Turks' and have been a driving force behind the organization of regular summit meetings be-

---

89 A. Arsharuni and Kh. Gabidullin, *Ocherki panislamizma i pantyurkizma v Rossii* (reprinted in London, Society for Central Asian Studies, 1990) presents a comprehensive survey of the subject, written from an early Soviet perspective.
90 Nursultan Nazarbayev, *A Strategy for the Development of Kazakhstan as a Sovereign State* (Washington DC, Kazakh Ministry of Foreign Affairs with Mercator Corporation, 1994), p. 57.

tween the leaders of the Turkic republics (the third was held in Bishkek in August 1995). Activities such as these have helped to foster the sense of a Turkic community of interests. Nevertheless, the Kazakhs, like the other Central Asians, are jealous of their newly acquired independence and are highly sensitive to any external attempts to impose new political or ideological constraints on their national policies. Cooperation with Turkey is welcomed, but in some circles the initial enthusiasm for rapprochement has been replaced by a degree of resentment at what is perceived to be the condescending 'neo-big brother' attitude of the Turks. There is also some disillusionment over Turkey's ability to provide financial aid and advanced technology; educational standards in Turkey have also often failed to live up to Kazakh expectations.[91] At the popular level, however, there is still a strong emotional attachment to Turkey; this is amplified by a growing number of personal contacts, including the reunification of family members, some of whom fled to China in the 1930s, then subsequently settled in Turkey. Considerably weaker is a sense of pan-Turkic unity within the Central Asian region. There are some individuals who espouse the creation (or recreation) of a united Turkestan, but they have no organized infrastructure. Moreover, there is an inherent conflict between Kazakh and Turkestani nationhood: in theory it might have been possible to create a unified Turkic/Turkestani entity in 1920, but now that separate national units have existed for 75 years, it is unlikely that such a project would be viable. What seems more probable is that Turkic-ness will remain an abstract marker of Kazakh identity, creating a predisposition towards cooperation within the larger Turkic community, but with only limited appeal as an active political force.

A third element, central to current perceptions of the national identity, is the elusive nomad legacy. As explained above, this does not survive as a living culture but it has left a powerful emotional and psychological imprint on the Kazakh population. Contemporary Kazakhs feel very strongly that they have their ethnic roots in a tradition that is markedly different from that of their sedentary neighbours and that consequently, in nature and outlook, they are a people apart. They trace their cultural and ethical values back to nomad traditions. The nomad way of life is now regarded with a respect that verges on nostalgic idealization. To some extent this preoccupation with a bygone age is an attempt to restore Kazakh self-esteem, so badly undermined under Soviet rule. It is also, however, a way of bridging the gulf between past and present. There is a considerable amount of wishful thinking in the attempts to ascribe to mod-

---

91 See, for example, the article by Azimbay Ghaliyev in the periodical *Ana Tili* (Almaty, 7 January 1993), quoted by D. Pipes, 'The Event of Our Era: Former Soviet Muslim Republics Change the Middle East', in M. Mandelbaum (ed.), *Central Asia and the World* (New York, Council on Foreign Relations Press, 1994), p. 55, in which the Kazakh scholar discusses at some length Turkey's weaknesses and concludes with the statement 'We must look at the Turkish example with critical eyes'. This is by no means an isolated example of current attitudes towards Turkey.

ern Kazakh society some of the perceived virtues of nomad life, but in a few spheres, notably in patterns of social behaviour, there is undoubtedly a certain degree of continuity. The highlighting of these features helps to lessen the sense of rootlessness and alienation from traditional culture that has characterized the Kazakh psyche for several decades.

Another reason for stressing the nomad legacy is that it represents a counterbalance to the Islamic tradition. During the Soviet period, the nomad component of Kazakh culture was given exclusive symbolic prominence in the newly crafted national identity (although in fact it had already been destroyed), while the Islamic element was dismissed, on the grounds that the Kazakhs were not 'real' Muslims, that their adherence to Islam was superficial and of recent date (arguments originally advanced by Shokan Valikhanov in the previous century). Today, 'Westernized' Kazakhs often use a similar line of reasoning to reassure their new international partners that, although they are Muslims, they are only nominally so, and that because of their nomad heritage, they will never be attracted by fundamentalist ideas. The nomad tradition is thus being used as a 'boundary marker' to differentiate Kazakhs from other Muslims, including neighbouring Central Asians, who are generally regarded (by the Kazakhs) as being more orthodox in their beliefs and practices. A further extension of this use of the nomad heritage to mark out a metaphoric national space is to emphasize the fact that it is a uniquely central Eurasian phenomenon, free of either the East or the West, although linked to both by cultural interchange, trade and transport networks: integrated, but independent – a neat reflection of the current foreign policy agenda.

The fourth element is a passionate attachment to the land. Sedentary peoples trace their history in durable, man-made monuments. The greatest achievement of the nomads, by contrast, was to leave as few marks as possible of their existence. Melding into the environment, they became an almost invisible part of the natural ecological cycle. Before the advent of the Russians, the Kazakhs had no maps of their territory because they needed none: every hill, lake and reed grove was clearly charted in their mental and spiritual picture of the region. This world has long since disappeared, but the land itself has come to constitute a link that is both symbolic and also physical between past and present. The bond is made all the stronger by the fact that the Kazakhs' forefathers are buried in this land; if the modern generation were to abandon it, it would amount to breaking faith with their ancestors. These are emotive arguments, no less powerful because they represent a modern, post-factum rationalization of Kazakh claims to the territory of present-day Kazakhstan. From a historical perspective, the geographic space was far from sacrosanct: apart from the major movements of population (which continued for centuries, in some cases even into the nineteenth century), proprietorial rights were very fluid and constantly in contention; it was the control of grazing lands, not graves, that was the chief motivation for gaining possession of the territory. If, however, it is accepted that there does exist a special bond between the people and the land, then logically, modern Kazakh territorial claims should extend to demands for the restitution of the parts of traditional 'Kazakh lands' that now lie outside the republic, in Russia and Uzbekistan. Such claims are not being made (at least not in public); such a course of action would not only present a major obstacle to good-neighbourly relations, but would certainly have no chance of success. The approach here is thus based on pragmatism rather than emotion.

To highlight this inconsistency is in no way to underestimate Kazakh sensitivities on the question of borders and the territorial integrity of the state. However, it is necessary to put these sentiments in context. The Kazakh preoccupation with territorial issues is not hard to understand: Kazakhstan is a country of great natural and industrial resources; it is also of major strategic importance. It covers a huge area (approximately five times the size of France), yet the total Kazakh population numbers less than 7 million. It is bordered by two powerful states, each of which could eventually have designs on Kazakh territory: China, a rapidly developing economy, in the throes of a virtually uncontrollable population explosion, might one day (it is feared) seek to expand westwards into the mineral-rich but sparsely populated Kazakh hinterland; Russia, impelled by nationalist motives, might seek to annex the Russian-populated northern regions, with their vast mineral and hydrocarbon reserves. Given that the Kazakhs have a minimal defence force (and even that is multi-ethnic and could not be relied upon in a clash with Russia), their sense of insecurity is understandable. It is only through the mobilization of domestic and international opinion to support their claim to this land that they can hope to hold onto it. Hence, the articulation of a 'primordial' right to the territory of Kazakhstan, although a genuine reflection of modern Kazakh perceptions, is also a political weapon to be wielded in defence of a highly vulnerable position.

The fundamental feature of modern Kazakh identity, that which underlies all other characteristics, is today rarely mentioned: namely, the Soviet legacy. The social engineering of the Soviet period has been discussed in Chapter 4. As indicated there, the socio-cultural changes that were introduced at this time were internalized to such a degree that they became an integral part of Kazakh life. This has created a gulf between the Kazakhs of Kazakhstan and the Kazakhs of China, Mongolia and elsewhere. The full extent of this divergence was not appreciated until, after independence, contacts were resumed between Kazakhs at home and abroad. At first there was great enthusiasm for the 'gathering-in' of the diaspora: Kazakhs from all over the world were welcomed at national and family reunions and urged to settle in the republic. Several thousand Kazakhs from Mongolia and Iran accepted this offer, but it soon became apparent that social, cultural and educational differences between the immigrants and the host population were so great that assimilation would be far from simple.

Immigration has since slowed to a trickle and some of the first settlers are indicating that they may not remain in Kazakhstan on a permanent basis. Closer links with the neighbouring Kazakhs of China (over a million in number) have similarly revealed substantial divergences between the two communities. Through these contacts, the Soviet legacy has come into sharper focus, distancing the Kazakhs who underwent Sovietization from those who did not.

Non-Kazakh minorities

Under Soviet rule, especially from the 1960s onwards, the Kazakhs, as the titular people of the republic, acquired a privileged position, with tacit priority status in a number of fields. Officially, however, they were on an equal par with the other ethnic groups. The bill on the sovereignty (in Soviet terminology, a lower level of autonomy than independence) of Kazakhstan, which was adopted on 25 October 1990, acknowledged the special position of the Kazakh people, but still only as that of first among equals. The 1993 Constitution went a stage further, specifying that the Republic of Kazakhstan, although it guaranteed equal rights to all its citizens, was founded on the principle of Kazakh national self-determination. Subsequently, the 1995 Constitution unequivocally designated the territory of the republic as primordial Kazakh land, thus giving an even clearer intimation of the move towards Kazakh ethnocracy. Yet the Kazakhs are still a minority within the state as a whole. The huge in-migration of Slav settlers at the turn of the century created a situation in which, even when the KASSR was created in 1920, the Kazakh population constituted less than 60 per cent of the total. Further waves of immigration during the Soviet period, as well as catastrophic population losses among the Kazakhs as a result of collectivization and sedentarization, almost halved their percentage share, lowering it to a mere 30 per cent by 1959; it slowly recovered thereafter and today stands at just over 44 per cent. The Slavs (Russians, Ukrainians and Byelorussians) constitute 42 per cent, the Germans almost 4 per cent, while Uzbeks, Tatars, Uighurs, Koreans, Jews, Poles and some 90 other ethnic groups are represented in much smaller numbers, together constituting 10 per cent of the population.

Some of these other groups have now been settled on the territory of modern Kazakhstan for several generations. The Slavs in particular feel that since they helped to cultivate the land, to protect its borders and to develop its trade and industry, they, too, should have a stake in the country and that this should be formally acknowledged in the institutions and symbols of the new state. In the immediate aftermath of the collapse of the Soviet Union it did seem as though this might be possible, since the President and other public figures promoted the concept of an inclusive 'Kazakhstani' identity. However, this ideal now appears to have been abandoned. The current con-

Ethnic Distribution c. 1994

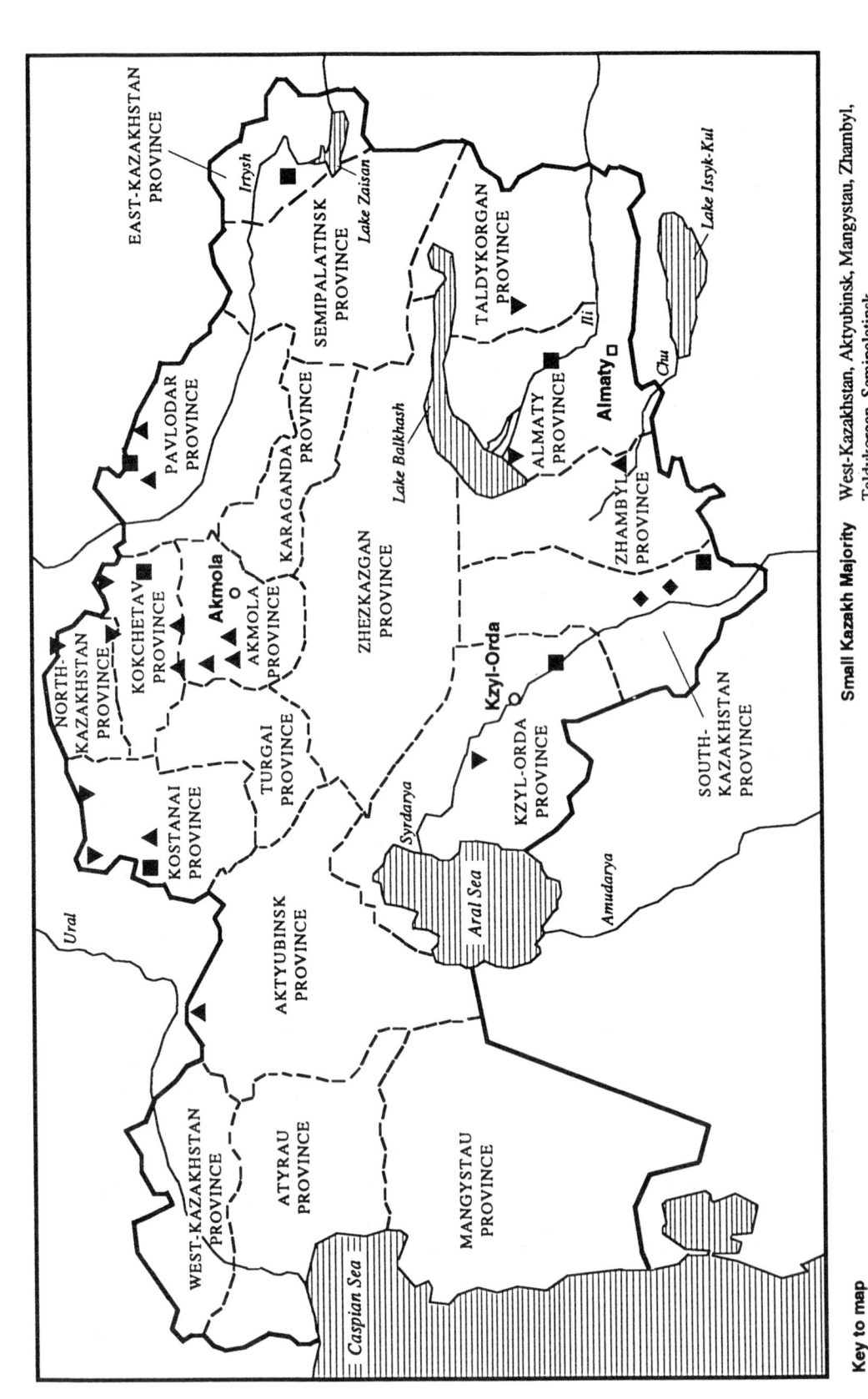

Key to map

Large Slav Majority — Kostanai, North-Kazakhstan, Karaganda.
Small Slav Majority — Kokchetav, Akmola, Pavlodar, East-Kazakhstan.
Mixed Slav-Kazakh — Turgai, Zhezkazgan, Almaty.
Small Kazakh Majority — West-Kazakhstan, Aktyubinsk, Mangystau, Zhambyl, Taldykorgan, Semipalatinsk.
Large Kazakh Majority — Kzyl-Orda, South-Kazakhstan, Atyrau.

▲ - Germans ▼ - Tatars ■ - Koreans ♦ - Uzbeks

stitution guarantees full citizenship rights for Kazakhs and non-Kazakhs alike, but the underlying implication is that the latter are foreigners who, for whatever reasons of their own, have chosen to settle on Kazakh territory and who must, therefore, accept the norms set by the titular nation. Some allowance is made by the state for the exercise of the cultural rights (including the establishment of cultural centres) of the non-Kazakh minorities, and Russian continues to be used as an official medium of communication, alongside Kazakh, the state language. However, these and other such provisions are regarded as concessions made by the 'majority' to the minorities. They do not constitute an attempt to develop a new Kazakhstani ethos, which would include, on an equal basis, the titular as well as the non-titular peoples of the republic; they emphasize, rather, the peripheral nature of the latter, and their subordinate status.

The suddenness of the transition from Soviet citizenship, which, despite enshrining Russian hegemony, was not officially ethnically specific, to Kazakh citizenship, which is unequivocally predicated on ethnic criteria, has inevitably been a disorienting experience, arousing feelings of intense insecurity amongst the non-Kazakhs. The situation has undoubtedly been exacerbated by the fact that on a personal, informal level, a number of Kazakhs are taking advantage of the situation to avenge past slights and injustices by a display of arrogance and racial discrimination; at times this verges on criminal harrassment of the European population. The increasing Kazakhification of all aspects of public life, evidenced by such trends as the growing use of the Kazakh language, the renaming of streets and cities, and the celebration of exclusively Kazakh cultural and historical events, has added to the sense of unease. The legal restrictions which were used to hamper Russian organizations from putting forward candidates in the parliamentary elections of March 1994 further increased concerns over officially condoned ethnic discrimination. Non-Kazakhs, already proportionally underrepresented in government and parliament,[92] fear a further decline in their political position, since the unspoken rule that is beginning to emerge is that key posts are given predominantly to Kazakhs. Despite official protestations to the contrary, it is regarded as no coincidence that by November 1994, less than three years after independence, the four highest offices of state (president, vice-president, prime minister and first deputy prime minister) were all held by Kazakhs.

The majority of the titular people are by no means ill-disposed towards the Slavs or other non-Kazakh minorities. However, they are still so concerned with the assertion of their own national independence that they frequently fail to grasp the full

---

92 In the parliamentary elections of March 1994, out of a total of 177 deputies, only 49 Russians, 10 Ukrainians, 3 Jews, 3 Germans and 6 representatives of other ethnic groups were elected; the remainder were all Kazakh. For a discussion of the 1995 constitutional crisis, see Sally Cummings, 'Politics in Kazakhstan: The Constitutional Crisis of March 1995', FSS Briefing No. 3, London, RIIA, August 1995.

extent of the psychological dislocation that their fellow citizens have suffered during the past few years. They genuinely regard it as a minor 'discomfort' that will soon evaporate, requiring no particular effort from their side to ease the situation. Some even see it as a test of allegiance that will remove those who are not fully committed to independent Kazakhstan. The non-Kazakh population, meanwhile, are becoming convinced that they have no future in Kazakhstan, that it is and will remain, as one commentator expressed it in June 1995, 'an apartheid state' in which there is institutionalized ethnic discrimination.[93] This has prompted a massive exodus of members of all the main non-Kazakh groups. In 1994 alone, over 400,000 people emigrated, nearly double the 1993 figure. This included over a quarter of a million Russians, nearly 90,000 Germans (the German population has been almost halved since 1989, when it numbered 958,000), over 30,000 Ukrainians, and almost 11,000 Tatars.[94]

The southern and western regions of Kazakhstan are now almost mono-ethnic, while even in the Karaganda and Akmola provinces there has been a substantial reduction in the non-Kazakh population. Demographic monitoring suggests that the next area to be so affected will be the Kostanai and North-Kazakhstan provinces. At the same time, there has been some in-migration of Kazakhs from Russia and from countries such as Mongolia and Iran (thousands of Kazakhs fled across these borders in the 1920s); the peak inflow was in 1993, when 23,490 Kazakhs returned to Kazakhstan.[95] Thus, although the Kazakh share in the population is still some way below the 50 per cent level, the movements of population, as well as the high birth-rate, seem likely to give them in the relatively near future an overall majority in the country as a whole, and a strong to almost complete domination of the south and centre, leaving enclaves of Slav concentrations along the Russian borders in the north-east and north-centre. These are the areas where there are strong Slav political organizations and a highly developed sense of Slav identity. This trend towards geographic ethnic consolidation is not conducive to the development of a cross-cultural dialogue. Rather, it is fostering isolationism and the polarization of the different communities. In the long term, this could be a serious threat to the territorial integrity of Kazakhstan, since not only are resentments being nurtured amongst the non-Kazakhs towards the titular people, but the physical and organizational conditions that would facilitate secession are being created. It is a situation that increasingly readily lends itself to exploitation by nationalists in Russia who believe that northern and eastern Kazakhstan are historically part of greater Russia.

---

93 The article by B. Ayaganov and A. Kuyandykov in *Aziya*, no. 29, June 1994, discusses this trend and concludes that these problems are arising because Kazakh self-awareness today is in a 'stress situation'.
94 *Kazakhstanskaya pravda*, 8 July 1995.
95 Ibid.

President Nazarbayev's role as inter-ethnic mediator

In the period immediately following the collapse of the Soviet Union President Nazarbayev was regarded by many – by foreign diplomats, CIS commentators and Kazakhs themselves – as the only person with the authority, negotiating skills and commitment to peaceful coexistence to be able to hold the country together, and to steer a smooth course towards liberal multi-party democracy. By 1994, however, enthusiasm for his domestic policies was beginning to wane. Abroad, foreign observers were disappointed by the practice of Soviet-style block voting in favour of the President and his nominees, while in Kazakhstan his handling of ethnic issues seemed vacillatory and he was accused of insincerity.

Too little is known of the inner workings of the higher echelons of government either during the Soviet period or today for an outsider to be able to comment with confidence, but from the available evidence it would seem that there is a considerable gap between the popular image of President Nazarbayev's position and the reality of the situation. His hold on power is both stronger and, paradoxically, weaker, than is often supposed. It is generally accepted that he is the only Kazakh with the training and experience to head a country with problems as complex and varied as those of Kazakhstan. That is indeed the case today, but was certainly not so in the late 1980s, when there were a number of other senior Kazakh party officials with similar talents, and enjoying a similar degree of public 'popularity' (if such a term has any validity in this context), among them M. S. Mendybayev and Z. K. Kamalidenov, to name but two. Once Nursultan Nazarbayev had secured the post of First Party Secretary in 1989, however, he deftly destroyed the power bases of these and all other potential rivals so that, when the Soviet Union collapsed, he was in truth the only person in place to take advantage of the new opportunities. The central government and the regional governments were already peopled with his supporters, officials who were loyal to him not only because his patronage had helped them in their careers, but because, by adhering to him, they could strengthen their own positions yet further. Thus the administrative system, which was where real power resided, was heavily weighted in President Nazarbayev's favour. By comparison, the new political parties were of very little significance. Weak and disorganized, they had no serious political programmes. Moreover, they had little following among the population, who, having been inoculated against party politics by the Communist Party of the Soviet era, looked on them all as vehicles for self-aggrandizement. Only a handful of individuals such as Olzhas Suleimenov, who had established a reputation in the pre-independence period, succeeded in winning any credibility whatsoever.

Against this background, the massive (though by no means unanimous) public support for President Nazarbayev, from Kazakhs as well as non-Kazakhs, is in no way surprising: he has a proven track record of competence, which, under present circumstances, is what is most in demand. This is where his strength lies. His weakness is that, like the Khans of old, he does not have the physical resources to impose his authority: he is able to govern, first, because he has the confidence of the overwhelming majority of the people, and secondly, because he has the tacit support of external agencies, governmental and non-governmental, who – whatever criticisms they may have of him – would prefer to see Nursultan Nazarbayev in office rather than some unknown and unpredictable figure. The most fickle of these two sources of support is undoubtedly that of the population. The President must constantly seek to keep their goodwill. He is sometimes accused by Western diplomats and other foreign observers of assuming dictatorial powers, but in fact, although he may manipulate parliament and the various political factions to his own advantage, ultimately he relies on achieving a consensus, with reciprocal benefits spread as widely as possible. In this sense Kazakhstan today is considerably more democratic than many of the other CIS members, although the democratic process itself, from a Western political perspective, is deeply flawed. The economic situation is still dire and there is little that can be done to bring about a rapid improvement. Satisfying national aspirations is considerably easier and he has been prepared to make a number of concessions in this direction. Yet even this requires a careful balancing act in order to avoid destabilization in some other area. In the negotiations over the relinquishing of the nuclear arsenal, for example, it was clear that the President's own instinct was to agree to the proposals put forward by the international community; the nationalist lobby, however, insisted that it would be a violation of the country's vital interests to surrender these weapons. There followed several months of anxious delay while the President worked to win round public opinion to support the denuclearization process.[96]

On ethnic issues Nazarbayev is likewise not a free agent. He may well be dismayed by the mass emigration of Russians, Germans and other non-Kazakhs, if only because of the damaging impact it is having on the economy. Nevertheless, he is unable to introduce the confidence-building measures which might reassure these minorities, since this could lose him support from the Kazakh population at a time when they are already suffering severe hardship as a result of the recession, and are likely to resent any assault on the one thing that the collapse of the Soviet Union has given them, namely, national independence. While the President has made several attempts to alleviate the concerns of the non-Kazakh minorities, he has not, in fact, succeeded in producing any long-term strategies on ethnic issues. Pragmatist that he is, his primary concern is to alleviate today's problems and, in the short term, the exodus of non-Kazakhs does represent a sort of solution: by removing the source of

---

96 Kazakhstan was formally declared 'nuclear-free' on 24 April 1995.

tension, it acts as a safety-valve, reducing the likelihood of immediate conflict. The future consequences of this trend, however, do not appear to be receiving any serious consideration.

Fragmentation in Kazakh society

During the Soviet period, fear of the centre helped to foster a sense of solidarity among the Kazakhs. Once this pressure was removed, the rifts in Kazakh society which were formerly almost invisible rapidly began to surface. One of these divisions is taking shape along regional lines. There are no major cultural or linguistic differences, but the sheer size of the country, with its huge expanses and sparse population, has always encouraged a centrifugal tendency towards local autonomy. During the Soviet period this was to some extent held in check, since the main locus of the centre–periphery power play was at the republican level, while that between the republican capital and the provinces was of secondary importance. Now, it is Almaty that represents the 'centre' and the struggle for local control has shifted to the provincial level. The fact that some of the provincial governments have on their territory mineral deposits of world-class interest has made them all the more eager to secure as much local control as possible. There is no move towards secession, but in at least some of the provinces the local elites are acquiring a high degree of *de facto* autonomy.

The regional divisions are sometimes interpreted as a re-emergence of the ancient Hordes. There is some superficial justification for such an assumption since, first, the chief territorial blocks correspond approximately to the 'economic units' which constituted the respective lands of the three Hordes; and secondly, over the past 50 years geographic mobility has been low, so in any given region the great majority of the local Kazakhs will be able to trace their ancestry back to the same Horde. Also, the dominant political and economic 'cliques', especially in provincial centres, will very probably be drawn from the same kin groups. Thus there is a certain congruence between past and present power and territorial groupings. This has prompted some 'outsiders', including, occasionally, Kazakhs who for one reason or another are excluded from a given group, to accuse such cliques of clan-horde solidarity. However, the idea that such clusters could form the basis of a reassertion of, say, Big Horde political supremacy is to misunderstand the nature of these structures. As discussed above, the neatly schematized clan-tribe-horde reconstructions of the early twentieth century are an idealized projection of how these formations ought to have functioned, omitting the reality of the constant changes of allegiance and fragmentation. It was precisely these internal stresses and weaknesses that caused the Hordes to implode some two hundred years ago; the clan-tribal hierarchies survived a little longer, in a somewhat modified fashion, but were heavily eroded in the course of the nineteenth century.

The fact that these units continue to have genealogical significance does not mean that this can be translated into an active socio-political force in today's world: to use the Scottish analogy again, a renascent Big Horde hegemony in Kazakhstan is as likely as that of a Clan MacDonald in Scotland. Quite apart from other considerations, the practice of exogamy alters family links and obligations from one generation to the next. It is almost impossible to find an individual with exclusive connections to any one of the Hordes. However, the idea that there might eventually be a 'Big Horde takeover' has taken root and is now fuelling a rash of conspiracy theories. It is becoming an addictive sport amongst Kazakh-watchers to pick out members of the ruling elite, past and present, who have a common Horde background. (Similar tactics have, of course, been used in other times and places; 'Zionist domination' theories are a case in point.) What is not being done, however, is to carry out an objective, systematic survey of the power structures to establish whether there is, over time, a real predominance of any one group and, more importantly, whether there is any indication that members of a given group have acted in concert to promote specific clan-horde interests. The available biographical evidence (admittedly incomplete) suggests that there is not, and has not been, such a plot. The proposed move of the capital from Almaty to Akmola, scheduled for the year 2000, is frequently explained as an attempt on the part of President Nazarbayev to break the supposed domination of Big Horde networks in the former city; the fact that the administration is likely to move *en masse* does not seem to figure in these calculations. Perhaps the most curious aspect of this whole furore is the passion with which the 'Horde conspiracy theory' is being embraced by Kazakhs who are close to Russian circles, in some cases resident in Moscow, in others associates of such organizations as *Russkaya obshchina* ('Russian Community'). Possibly this is another example of a Russian interpretation of 'primitive' Kazakh society being uncritically adopted by Russified Kazakhs.

A less obvious, but in the long term perhaps more serious, gulf is that which is emerging between the affluent Kazakhs of the cities and the poorer, more conservative population of the rural central and southern provinces. The former, the Russian-speaking and Russian-educated minority, are now increasingly at home in the capitals of the world, part of the international business and diplomatic community. The latter, primarily Kazakh-speakers, adhere to traditional customs (for example, with regard to gender roles) and have little experience of life outside their immediate settlement. They have suffered most from the disintegration of the Soviet Union, which has resulted in a cut in welfare subsidies, a deterioration in rural health services and a fall in educational standards. They feel alienated and excluded from the prosperity that independence has brought to the business and government elites. The more vehemently nationalistic of the urban Kazakhs identify strongly with the plight of the rural poor, whom they regard as the living repository of Kazakh culture. They believe that the government's priority should be to improve conditions in the deprived areas of the south and centre. If the development gulf continues to widen (as at present it seems likely to do), it could well, in time, lead to a north-south split. The urbanized Kazakhs of the industrial north might, under such conditions, feel more strongly attracted to the Slav fringe, finding there a community of economic interests of sufficient power to outweigh the ethnic pull to the south.

A third form of fragmentation is the horizontal layering that is arising out of ever-widening wealth differentials. This has its roots in the general economic dislocation, but has been given greater emphasis by the privatization process. As during the 1930s, when collectivization was imposed by decree from above (a comparison that is often made in the Kazakh press), there has been a chaotic scramble to produce satisfactory statistics; in reality, the programme has, from the outset, been mired in incompetence, poor organization and corruption, and the actual achievements are far more modest than official estimates would suggest.[97] Once again, as in the 1930s, greed for property and power has become a dominant factor. Loyalties within the immediate family unit are still generally strong, but beyond that circle there is little sense of solidarity. Extra-familial networks, held together by bonds of professional 'usefulness', are far more effective agencies for gaining control of lucrative enterprises than are the vertical chains of kin-based networks. Arguably, since independence a greater degree of reorganization has taken place in Kazakh society than at any time during the preceding half-century. Personal observation and anecdotal evidence both suggest that today, although there may be some notional concept of social responsibility to the extended family unit, in practice peer group loyalties are gaining priority and are helping to strengthen the new economic stratification. Vested interests are now no longer located in 'traditional' clan groupings but in the emerging commercial structures. There may be much that is beneficial in this process, but there is also the danger that it will lead to a two-nation split between rich and poor, which, at this early stage of national consolidation, could prove to be an additional threat to stability.

Friends and enemies

The disintegration of the Soviet Union necessitated a reappraisal of the Kazakhs' relationship with their immediate neighbours, and also with the wider international community. The inherited perception of most Kazakhs was that they were surrounded by enemies, many of whom possessed, or soon might possess, nuclear weapons. Those

---

[97] See *Central Asia Newsfile*, no. 9, July 1993, in which it was reported that Z. Karibzhanov, Head of the State Property Committee, had announced that many of the 6,200 privatizations that had been carried out to date had had to be cancelled because of irregularities of various sorts.

who aroused the greatest fear at this point were: (1) the Chinese, who had long been portrayed as the traditional foe of the Kazakhs; (2) the Iranians, represented as fanatical Muslim fundamentalists intent on establishing an Islamic state in Central Asia; and (3) the Americans and west Europeans, caricatured as rapacious aggressors eager to exploit the natural resources of the region. However, once direct contact had been established with these and other countries, the Kazakh government soon came to realize that they did not, in fact, pose any immediate threat and that, on the contrary, they could be valuable economic partners. As more foreigners came to live and work in the republic, so, too, the general public began to shed the prejudices and inhibitions that had been inherited from the Soviet era. Friendly relations were established with many Middle Eastern countries, notably Iran, Egypt and the Gulf states, and also Israel; new links were forged with the Far East and Southeast Asia, especially with Korea, Malaysia and Thailand; and a good working partnership was developed with west European countries, Turkey, the United States, Canada and Australia. Many Kazakhs are now studying in these countries. China is still regarded with a degree of suspicion, but outstanding border issues have been resolved amicably and bilateral trade and economic cooperation are flourishing; the ongoing programme of nuclear tests at Lop Nor, not far from the border with Kazakhstan, remains a cause of grave concern to the Kazakhs, but links have been established with the Chinese Ministry of Defence and a dialogue is in progress on this subject. This diversification of international contacts has helped to sharpen Kazakh self-awareness: there is now a greater sense of what is unique in Kazakh culture, outlook and aspirations, and also of what is shared with others. A common sense of Islamic identity, for example, provides a useful foundation on which to develop links with Muslim countries, but at the same time, closer contacts with the latter have shown the Kazakhs that contemporary Islam is by no means monolithic, and that their own understanding of Islam may at times vary greatly from that of others. Links with the Far East and Southeast Asia have revealed unexpected similarities in cultural propensities; these are given incidental, but psychologically not insignificant, support by the strong physical similarities between Kazakhs and the peoples of the Far East.

The relationship with neighbouring members of the CIS has been more complicated. Kazakhstan remains tightly bound to Russia by innumerable horizontal links, including joint defence programmes, transport networks and intermeshed industries. The two countries share a long common border and there are some 6 million Russians still resident in Kazakhstan; moreover, Russian culture and the Russian language are still very important to many Kazakhs, especially in the northern belt. There are, too, bonds of personal friendship and trust, and a fund of shared experiences. It is a relationship that has been forged in the course of almost two centuries and cannot easily be dismantled. However, despite all the undoubted mutual warmth and dependency, there is an acute awareness that the most serious threat to the economic and territorial independence of Kazakhstan is posed by Russia. Thus, while on the one hand there is a desire for continuing cooperation, there is also a need to pull away, to establish real as well as metaphorical boundaries. The insistence on Kazakh national symbols and on Kazakh as the national language are symptomatic of this drive to negotiate a space between the two states and the two cultures.

The relationships with the adjacent states of Uzbekistan, Kyrgyzstan and Turkmenistan are likewise based on genuine links of friendship and an acknowledged community of interests, but are also complicated by historic animosities and current economic rivalries. Steps are being taken to create viable regional institutions and the current intention is that Uzbekistan, Kazakhstan and Kyrgyzstan should form an economic union, possibly as a prelude to political union. There are, however, potential territorial claims and counter-claims which Uzbekistan and Kazakhstan could make against each other; these could be reinforced by the manipulation of irredentist aspirations among the large cross-border minority groups of Uzbeks and Kazakhs respectively. Both countries insist that they intend to respect the present frontiers, but in that very insistence there is an implicit awareness that today's avowals will not necessarily be honoured tomorrow. For the present, however, there are no outstanding areas of disagreement and the current trend is to minimize past grievances and to stress, instead, common origins.

7 CONCLUSION

Current trends

Two trends are emerging in Kazakh society: one is nationalist, the other 'internationalist' (in the Soviet sense of harmonious inter-ethnic relations) in orientation. However, in both the public and the private spheres, at government level and at the level of the individual, there is an almost schizophrenic oscillation between these two positions. Thus, the most ardent nationalist may suddenly espouse an 'internationalist' stance, or vice versa, depending on the issue and the context. The nationalist camp encompasses a wide range of views and priorities, ranging from Kazakh cultural rehabilitation to a radical 'Kazakhstan for the Kazakhs' agenda. Adherents of the latter position favour the mass emigration of all non-Kazakhs, even if this results in serious damage to the economy. There is no formally constituted nationalist movement. Oppostion groups such as Alash and Azat often indulge in provocatively nationalist rhetoric, mainly as a means of attracting attention, but they do not have any specific programmes of their own. They do, however, provide a conduit for the expression of ultranationalist sentiments, thereby contributing to a general radicalization of public opinion. Extremist nationalist views are still condemned in public, but in private they are greeted with a certain amount of sympathy.

The 'internationalist' camp recognizes the need to protect Kazakh culture, but is opposed to the isolationist stance of the nationalists. Its proponents stress the need for social stability within the republic, seeing this as the prerequisite for realizing Kazakhstan's rich human and material potential. Some are even prepared to contemplate an increase in mass immigration, not simply of Kazakhs from abroad, but of people of all ethnic origins, in emulation of the policies of countries such as Canada and Australia which have similar problems of a huge territory, vast mineral wealth and a comparatively small population. Those who favour the 'internationalist' trend tend to be well-educated, urban-based professionals who are involved in some branch of the burgeoning new enterprise culture. They are economically powerful and are beginning to exert some political leverage on the government. Within the Kazakh population as a whole, however, they are a small minority.

Caught between these two groups is a body of bewildered people, who, unable to come to terms with the upheavals of recent years, still regard themselves as Soviet citizens, albeit of Kazakh nationality. Their primary concerns are not political platforms, but food, medical care, transport and education. They are for the most part voiceless, unrepresented in the debates in parliament, the media and the public rallies. It is impossible to estimate accurately the size of this group, or its geographic distribution. Personal observations and conversations indicate that such views are typical of the smaller provincial towns and settlements in the sparsely populated southern and central regions; they are also widespread amongst middle-level professionals in urban areas. These people constitute the backbone of the support for the government, and specifically for President Nazarbayev, who, for them, represents a guarantee of continuity and stability. Nevertheless, even amongst this otherwise apolitical group, a streak of xenophobia is surfacing, providing fertile ground for nascent nationalism.

Outlook

The reformulation of post-Soviet Kazakh identity is still at an early, inchoate stage. The Kazakhs of today have only just embarked on the process of reinterpreting a history and culture that is fraught with fracture and ambiguity, with great achievements that are inextricably linked with great tragedies. This process is not taking place in a vacuum, under conditions of impartial academic scrutiny, but at a time of profound social and economic change. New imperatives are arising even as the old are being discarded. For the first time in modern history, the Kazakhs constitute an independent political entity, within internationally recognized state borders. They are the masters of their own destiny to a greater extent than at any time in the past 250-odd years. At the same time, they have also, suddenly and unexpectedly, acquired a degree of control over, and responsibility for, a large number of non-Kazakh minorities. The relationship with these groups, quite as much as the rediscovery of their past, will influence the future development of the Kazakh national identity – or even multiple national identities. If narrowly nationalistic sentiments come to predominate, they will inevitably lead to ethnic confrontation, and possibly even to the dismemberment of the state. If a more tolerant attitude prevails, one which allows for the full expression of Kazakh aspirations but without reducing non-Kazakhs to the status of second-class citizens, then there is every possibility that the different groups will succeed in working together for their mutual benefit. A more broadly-based, pluralistic 'Kazakhstani' identity might then emerge.

Nowhere in the world has the management of multi-ethnic states, especially those which have a bilingual divide, proved to be a simple matter: whether in Fiji or Canada, Malaysia or Belgium, conflicting ethnic interests and linguistic sensibilities have caused serious strains. Kazakhstan has, up to now, had little experience of these problems. Since independence, however, they have begun to surface. For the present, the situation is still in flux and it is impossible to predict not only the outcome, but how long it will take for this transitional stage to assume a more permanent form.

Nevertheless, a knowledge of the historical background can help to clarify the issues that are shaping the current situation, and that are likely to play a decisive role in the future. The dilemmas of identity and self-perception that confront the Kazakhs today have their roots in the past. Likewise the relationship between Kazakhs and non-Kazakhs, especially that with the Russians, cannot be fully comprehended unless viewed in a perspective that extends back over centuries. History does not provide answers for the future, but it does sometimes illuminate our understanding of the present, offering explanations for phenomena that might otherwise seem arbitary and unmotivated. In the case of Kazakhstan it is particularly important to penetrate beneath the surface of current events, since the rhetoric and emotion of the post-Soviet discourse is not necessarily an accurate guide to more fundamental developments in society. These are driven not only by present circumstances, but are also a response to the historical legacy. The future of both the Kazakh nation and the Kazakh state will thus in large measure depend on the conduct of this process of coming to terms with the past.

FURTHER READING

R. Altoma, 'The Influence of Islam in Post-Soviet Kazakhstan' in B. F. Manz (ed.), *Central Asia in Historical Perspective* (Boulder CO, Westview Press, 1994), pp. 164-81.

A. Bodger, 'Change and Tradition in Eighteenth-Century Kazakhstan: The Dynastic Factor', in S. Akiner (ed.), *Cultural Change and Continuity in Central Asia* (London, Kegan Paul International, 1991), pp. 344-60.

M. Brill Olcott, *The Kazakhs* (Stanford, Hoover Institution Press, 1987).

G. J. Demko, *The Russian Colonisation of Kazakhstan 1896-1916* (Bloomington IN, Indiana University Press, 1969).

M. Mandelbaum (ed.), *Central Asia (Kazakhstan, Uzbekistan, Tajikistan, Kyrgyzstan, Turkmenistan) and the World* (New York, Council on Foreign Relations Press, 1994).

N. Melvin, *Russians Beyond Russia: The Politics of National Identity* (London, Pinter for the RIIA, 1995), Chapter 6.